Geography Mysteries

Dynamic Learning Adventures

by Marjorie Frank

Illustrated by Kathleen Bullock

Incentive Publications, Inc.
Nashville, Tennessee

To Teachers and Parents

- Use each geography mystery as a short warm-up to stimulate social studies exploration and reasoning, and to build excitement about geography. OR use any one as the basis for a longer geography lesson focused on the related topic, concept, or process.

- Use the mysteries randomly. OR choose one that specifically fits a concept or standard—to introduce, review, or sharpen understanding and application of that concept.

- Use the mysteries to complement any social studies course. The geographic knowledge, research skills, and thinking processes involved in these mysteries are used in ALL fields of social studies.

- Student "detectives" will need geography tools for most of the mysteries. Have plenty of world maps, globes, atlases, and other map resources available. It will also be helpful for students to have access to an up-to-date world almanac, a good encyclopedia, and the Internet.

- Always take time for students to ponder strategies for solving the mystery. Encourage them to discuss the steps they will take (or took), and the reasons for their answers or solutions. Ask them to share new information they learned while solving the mystery.

- Help students connect the concepts and processes of each mystery to their real lives. Ask them to think of places and times they have seen or used the same kind of process, information, idea, or result.

Notes:

- The tables on pages 5 to 7 list geography topics, concepts, themes, standards, and processes sharpened by the mysteries. These will help you find an activity connected to a specific standard, concept, or skill.

- Pages 106 and 107 contain suggestions for teaching strategies to help you lead students to gain deeper understandings and make relevant connections for geography concepts.

- Make available copies of the World Time Zone Map on page 108 for solving mysteries that involve time zones.

Illustrated by Kathleen Bullock
Cover design by Debbie Weekly
Edited by Joy MacKenzie

ISBN 978-0-86530-528-1

1   2   3   4   5   6   7   8   9   10   14   13   12   11

Printed by Sheridan Books, Inc., Chelsea, Michigan • June 2011
www.incentivepublications.com

What do you get when you mix a curious, clever rat with interesting places around the world and a host of tangled geography mysteries? You get dozens of dilemmas that need application of sharp social studies concepts and reasoning skills—plus a whole lot of adventuresome fun!

Captivated by Geography

Join Rosco Rat and his band of independent (and slightly quirky) friends as they encounter all kinds of quandaries at home and around the world.

- With his sharp brain and keen street-survival skills, Rosco is a natural at good detecting and problem solving. He likes to snoop around; find tidbits of information (along with tidbits of food); and draw conclusions about people, events, places, and situations.

- This book is full of surprises, humor, delightful cartoons, and intrigue. You'll be invited to help Rosco solve some very unusual mysteries. To do this, you will need to use your best skills of inquiry and reasoning—because these are essential to good mystery investigation.

- Have fun combining your curiosity, ingenuity, reasoning skills, map skills, and geography knowledge as you track down culprits, catch suspects, find your way to various places on the globe, and locate missing things or persons.

CONTENTS

To the Student:
Let the Mysteries Begin!

About the Mysteries

- Each activity starts with a curious story that sets the stage for a mystery. This introduction includes some details or clues related to the situation.

- Then the mystery is stated in the form of a question or instruction to find something or come to some conclusion. To solve the mystery, apply the geography information you know, research to find any information you do not have, and find the right map to help you locate and compare places.

- Then use your best reasoning to apply all that information to arrive at a solution. Think outside ordinary boundaries, be willing to ask questions, combine your previous knowledge with your cleverest ideas, and venture a solution for the mystery.

How to Use this Book

- Read each mystery all the way through. Identify tools that will help you get the information needed (maps, globe, measuring tools, encyclopedias, almanac, and such). Gather these supplies before you begin.

- You can tackle a geography mystery alone, but sometimes it is fun to work with a partner or small group. Get someone to join you in pondering the question or doing the research—especially if you are having trouble with a particular mystery.

- With each mystery, try to identify the big idea(s) of geography and the processes that you will use to find a solution.

- When you reach a solution for the mystery, explain how you found it. Compare your solution and strategies with someone else's.

- When you finish each one, make note of something new you learned about geography while you figured out the answer to the mystery question.

- All of these mysteries will stretch your brain. Have fun trying them out. And have fun with Rosco and friends!

Geography Topics and Concepts Supported by the Mysteries

Skill, Concept, or Process	Mystery Number(s)
Earth's revolution, rotation, tilt, hemispheres, continents, major lines of latitude and longitude	19, 21, 38, 41, 42, 52, 56, 60, 67, 71, 72, 78, 83, 87
World regions	1, 4, 7, 8, 9, 10, 12, 18, 19, 22, 23, 28, 30, 34, 36, 38, 41, 44, 46, 47, 48, 53, 54, 55, 62, 65, 66, 69, 80
World nations	1, 6, 7, 8, 9, 11, 12, 13, 20, 23, 25, 26, 27, 30, 34, 35, 39, 44, 47, 53, 54, 55, 56, 57, 58, 60, 61, 62, 63, 69, 74, 75, 76, 79, 83, 84
World cities, capital cities	1, 2, 5, 9, 23, 39, 46, 53, 54, 57, 60, 75, 83
USA and Canada, political and natural features	5, 8, 14, 18, 20, 26, 32, 51, 66, 72, 73, 82
Geographic terms and features	5, 9, 11, 16, 17, 20, 25, 26, 30, 31, 32, 33, 36, 38, 42, 50, 52, 54, 55, 58, 62, 64, 65, 66, 71, 72, 76, 77, 78, 61, 84, 86, 87
Landforms	11, 13, 20, 22, 25, 26, 30, 31, 32, 33, 36, 38, 42, 49, 50, 52, 54, 55, 58, 62, 64, 65, 66, 77, 78, 86
Bodies of water	5, 9, 17, 20, 26, 28, 31, 33, 36, 42, 44, 49, 52, 54, 55, 63, 66, 69, 71, 72, 77, 78, 81, 84, 86, 87
Climate, weather, biomes, wildlife, vegetation	11, 27, 28, 38, 49, 60, 63, 65, 70, 79
Earth processes	30, 63
Latitude and longitude locations	1, 2, 5, 29, 38, 56, 61, 71, 72, 75, 79, 83, 87
Time Zones, time lines, time questions	5, 6, 10, 39, 43, 51, 56, 74, 79, 80
Historical features	4, 14, 29, 32, 35, 41, 76 , 89
Cultural and economic features, developments, and attractions	3, 4, 10, 12, 14, 19, 25, 32, 35, 41, 46, 63, 64, 67, 68, 76, 78, 80, 82, 88
Interaction of physical and human systems	1, 3, 12, 14, 25, 29, 32, 35, 40, 46, 47, 60, 67, 76, 78, 80, 81, 89
Research skills: research using resources other than maps	4, 7, 8, 10, 11, 12, 13, 14, 16, 17, 20, 22, 27, 28, 29, 30, 33, 36, 37, 41, 42, 43, 45, 46, 49, 57, 60, 63, 65, 67, 68, 72, 73, 75, 79, 82, 88, 89, 90
Map skills: find directions and distances on maps	1, 3, 6, 8, 9, 14, 15, 18, 20, 23, 24, 40, 44, 51, 53, 54, 56, 57, 58, 62, 69, 70, 85, 86, 89
Map skills: use maps to locate places and to compare locations	1, 2, 3, 5, 6, 7, 8, 9, 13, 14, 17, 18, 19, 20, 21, 22, 23, 24, 25, 26, 29, 30, 31, 32, 33, 34, 35, 37, 38, 40, 41, 44, 45, 47, 48, 51, 52, 53, 54, 55, 56, 57, 58, 59, 61, 62, 64, 65, 66, 68, 69, 70, 71, 72, 73, 74, 76, 77, 78, 79, 80, 81, 82, 83, 84, 85, 86, 87, 89, 90
Map skills: Use a variety of maps to find information: elevation, grid, floor plan, road, political, natural features, time zone. Use map features: titles, compass, key, labels, scale.	all mysteries

National Geography Standards Supported by the Mysteries

(Core Standards from the National Council on Geographic Education)

Element	Standard # and Description
The World in Spatial Terms	1 How to use maps and other geographic representations, tools, and technologies to acquire, process, and report information from a spatial perspective 2 How to use mental maps to organize information about people, places, and environments in a spatial context 3 How to analyze the spatial organization of people, places, and environments on Earth's surface
Places and Regions	4 The physical and human characteristics of places 5 That people create regions to interpret Earth's complexity
Physical Systems	8 The characteristics and spatial distribution of ecosystems on Earth's surface
Human Systems	9 The characteristics, distribution, and migration of human populations on Earth's surface 10 The characteristics of Earth's cultural mosaics 12 The patterns of human settlement 14 How human actions modify the physical environment
Environment and Society	15 How physical systems affect human systems

Five Themes of Geography Supported by the Mysteries

(Framework for Teaching Geography, National Council on Geographic Education)

1. **Place**—the uniqueness of a place on Earth. This includes the physical characteristics of the land, water, plants, animals, climate, soil, and natural resources. It also includes the cultural characteristics: the people—their social, cultural, and economic practices and traditions and their relationship with the land.

2. **Location**—the specific spot where something can be found. This includes the absolute location (the exact spot) and the relative location—the relationship of one person, place or thing in comparison to some other spot.

3. **Human and Environment Interaction**—the connection between the physical environment and the way people live and the way cultures develop. This also includes the effects that humans have on the physical environment.

4. **Human Movement**—the patterns of and reasons for movement of groups of people. This includes the study of movement of ideas, information, and goods.

5. **Regions**—areas of the earth's surface defined by unifying characteristics. These characteristics may be physical, human, or cultural. Geographers are also interested in how regions change over time.

Thinking Skills Supported by the Mysteries

Structure Based on Bloom's Taxonomy of Cognitive Development

Cognitive Domain Levels *Simplest* ➝ *Most Complex*	Skills	Mystery Number(s)
Remembering: Recall data or information	arrange, define, describe, duplicate, label, list, match, name, order, recall, recognize, repeat, reproduce, select, state	Mysteries 1-90
Understanding: Understand the meaning, translation, interpolation, and interpretation of instructions and problems. Explain concepts and state a problem in one's own words	classify, describe, discuss, explain, express, identify, indicate, locate, recognize, report, select, translate, paraphrase	Mysteries 1-90
Applying: Use a concept in a new situation or unprompted use of an abstraction	apply, choose, demonstrate, dramatize, employ, illustrate, interpret, operate, practice, schedule, sketch, solve, use, write	Mysteries 1-90
Analyzing: Distinguish among component parts to arrive at meaning or understanding	analyze, appraise, calculate, categorize, compare, contrast, criticize, differentiate, discriminate, distinguish, examine, experiment, question, test	Mysteries 1-90
Evaluating: Justify a decision or position; make judgments about the value of an idea	appraise, argue, assess, defend, evaluate, judge, rate, select, support, value, compose, construct, create, design, develop, formulate, manage, organize, plan, set up, prepare, propose, write	Mysteries 1-90
Creating: Create a new product or viewpoint	assemble, construct, create, design, develop, formulate, mold, prepare, propose, synthesize, write	Mysteries 8, 10, 16, 33, 35, 80, 90

Doing Geography the Brain-Compatible Way

For students to be skilled at geography, they must be able to do far more than remember the names and locations of continents, oceans, and countries. Geography requires deep understandings of the physical world and its relationship to human societies and systems. Middle level students of geography will need to combine factual knowledge with more complex processes of questioning, researching, making connections, analyzing, and drawing conclusions.

Brain-compatible learning theory is based on information that neuroscientists have learned about how the brain perceives, senses, processes, stores, and retrieves information. Brain-based learning principles offer useful strategies for learning geography in ways that cement understanding and fix concepts in long-term memory.

Social science understandings are deepened when the concept, problem, or process is . . .

- connected to art, visuals, graphics, or color.

- presented with humor.

- related to real-life experiences and problems.

- presented in a setting in which you can be involved in DOING.

- presented in a setting in which you are invited to give feedback about it.

- connected to or learned in the context of a strong emotion.

- presented in a way that engages you personally.

- used in a variety of forms and manipulated in a variety of ways.

- applied to other situations with which you are already familiar.

- relevant to your interests and your life.

- used in situations where you are asked to explain (with writing, illustration, speaking, or otherwise) how you are thinking about it, how and why it works, how you have used it, and what it means.

- presented in a way that asks you to apply it to new or unexpected problems and situations.

- used settings where you discuss, share, explain, and demonstrate it with others.

- learned or applied in an environment that is relatively free from stress and threat.

The
90
Geography Mysteries

The Long-Distance Pizza

Though Roso Rat loves the normal routine of roaming his own city (with special attention to garbage cans and dumpsters), his natural spirit of adventure also lures him to faraway places. As he visits cities, countries, and waters across the world, he often finds himself in the middle of a mystery. Because of his natural cleverness and sharp mind, he can't resist stopping to follow a suspect, catch a thief, or untangle a tricky case.

Right now, he's off to solve a mystery that is very near to his heart (and stomach). He's headed for the capital city of a country rumored to have the best cheese pizza in the world. And if there's any pizza left after he samples it, he's promised to bring some back home to his friends in New York City.

Follow the clues to solve the mystery.

Clues:

- The capital city is on a coastline.

- The city is farther south than another national capital, Bogata.

- The city is farther north than Pretoria.

- It lies in two hemispheres different from those where Ottawa is located.

- It is farther west than Wellington.

- It is farther east than Tokyo.

- This capital's nation shares an island with land from another nation.

I CAN ALMOST SMELL PIZZA FROM HERE!

The Mystery:

AT WHICH WORLD CAPITAL DID ROSCO FIND THE PIZZA?

Name_____

10

Follow the Macaroni

May 1

Rosco follows his nose
to a little cafe located at
about **35°S, 58°W.**

WHERE IS ROSCO?

The lure of good macaroni and cheese sends Rosco
off to big cities around the world searching for more
of his favorite cheese dish.

The latitude and longitude descriptions give precise
locations of the places Rosco visits by boat, plane,
train, or on foot. Identify each city where he tastes
macaroni and cheese. (Of course, he does far more
than just taste!)

May 5

Ocean breezes bring
the scent of yummy cheese
to tickle Rosco's nose
at this location:
34°S, 151°E.

WHERE IS ROSCO?

May 8

The noisy streets of this
city at about **6°S, 106°E**
do not distract Rosco
from his quest.

WHERE IS ROSCO?

ANOTHER HELPING
OF MACARONI AND
CHEESE SUPREME,
PLEASE.

ROSCO

The Mystery:

WHERE IS ROSCO ON
EACH OF THESE DAYS?

May 14

On his way to eat creamy macaroni
at about **18°N, 77°W**, Rosco stops to
shake his tail to reggae music.

WHERE IS ROSCO?

May 18

He may hear over 200 different
languages spoken in this capital
city located at about **4°S, 15°E.**
It's a good thing Rosco understands
"cheese" in any language.

WHERE IS ROSCO?

May 22

This latest casserole of mac
and cheese is so rich, creamy,
and plentiful that Rosco can not
move after eating this batch.
So he just stays here for
a long, long time—at a location
of about **41°N, 14°E.**

WHERE IS ROSCO?

Name_____

The Fraudulent Paintings

While Rosco is in Paris eating macaroni, a fraud is discovered at the Louvre Museum. A priceless painting, *le grand fromage qui pue*, has been replaced by a copy. Versions of this painting are hidden at several Parisian landmarks. An anonymous call tips police to the locations and the clue that one of these is the masterpiece.

● Rosco tags along with police as they pick up paintings at these sites featured on the map:

    a) directly east of Musée du Louvre

    b) northwest of Parc des Buttes-Chaumont

    c) on island in Seine River

    d) directly southeast of La Sorbonne

    e) farthest west on Les Champs Elysées

    f) just north of Boulevard Périphérique

● Of the paintings retrieved, the one hidden farthest from Parc Citroën is the original.

Key for Sites

1 Sacré-Coeur
2 L'Arc de Triomphe
3 Tour Eiffel
4 Musée du Louvre
5 Palais Royale
6 Place de la Bastille
7 Notre Dame
8 La Sorbonne
9 Pantheon
A Parc Citroën
B Parc des Buttes-Chaumont
C Parc Montsouris

The Mystery:

AT WHICH FAMOUS SITE IN PARIS IS THE REAL PAINTING HIDDEN?

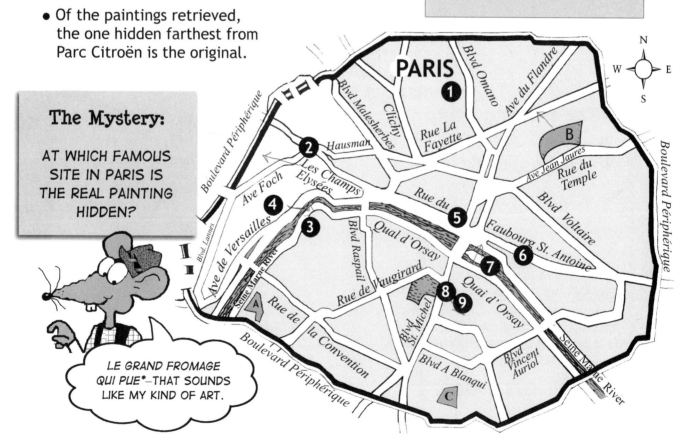

LE GRAND FROMAGE QUI PUE*—THAT SOUNDS LIKE MY KIND OF ART.

*THE GREAT SMELLY CHEESE

Name_____

The Hidden Artifacts

As Rosco searches London for new taste sensations, he gets word that a valuable artifact, given as a gift to the queen, has been smuggled out of the palace and may be hidden in one of the guard's tall hats. Rosco may look like an ordinary tourist, but his sharp eyes watch for suspicious behavior.

This smuggled artifact is one of the following:

- bronze statue of a Mesopotamian goddess
- piece of obsidian pottery from Sardinia
- Samurai dagger
- pre-Columbian Aztec mask
- tiny Tang Dynasty vase
- Greek terra-cotta figurine
- scrap of a priceless Persian tapestry

The missing artifact originally came from a place near a large peninsula, a sea, a large gulf, a mountain range, and countries such as present-day Iraq, Iran, and Syria.

THERE'S DEFINITELY SOMETHING SUSPICIOUS HERE!

The Mystery:

WHICH OF THE SEVEN ARTIFACTS COULD BE HIDDEN UNDER A GUARD'S HAT?

Name_____

Vacation by the Sea

Rosco has invited Boomerang to join him on an island vacation. The cat has no idea where this island will be—and he is not thrilled by the name of the island. But he's excited about the chance to do a little fishing!

Rosco and Boomerang leave New York City and fly directly east for 11 hours. After doing a little island hopping, they end up at a resort on a sea that is just about the same latitude as New York City. The sea is bordered by six countries, with a strait that opens on the south end to another, smaller sea.

The Mystery:

WHAT SEA CAN THEY SEE FROM THEIR BEACHFRONT RESORT?

Name_____

14

Race Against Time

At 5:00 PM on Tuesday, Rosco was sampling sushi in Hong Kong. Meanwhile in Somalia, a rare, poisonous insect had just stung his good friend, Boomerang. Rosco immediately mobilized to help. His challenge would be to pick up a sample of blood from the victim, fly it to a lab in Brazil where an antidote would be made, and get it back to Somalia within 48 hours of the sting—if he wanted to save his friend's life.

- Rosco got the news and hurried to the airport. He was able to leave Hong Kong at 7:00 PM Hong Kong time—two hours after the incident.

- His flight to Mogadishu, Somalia arrived at 9:00 PM Somalia time.

- It took four hours to hire a small plane, get to the site of the incident, get back to the airport, and be on time to board another plane.

- This flight landed in Manaus, Brazil Wednesday at 8:00 AM Manaus time.

- Rosco waited in Manaus for the antidote to be made and delivered to him. He was able to leave the ground just two hours after the time he arrived.

- The flight back to Somalia took thirteen hours. After he arrived, another two hours passed before Rosco could reach Boomerang.

The Mystery:

WHEN DID ROSCO REACH BOOMERANG WITH THE ANTIDOTE?

DID THIS HAPPEN IN TIME TO SAVE HIS FRIEND?

Name_____

The Nacho Nabber

Rosco stumbled upon the nacho dish of his dreams at a little shack in Puerto San Jose, Guatemala. Just as he was sitting outside relishing in the ecstasy of his discovery, a nacho bandit was slinking out the back door with a batch of nachos and the secret recipe.

Local law enforcement officers chased the nacho nabber to a string of cities throughout Central and South America.

They tracked him from Tegucigalpa , Honduras

✓ TO LEÓN , Nicaragua

   TO CASTRIES , St. Luria

✓ TO VALENCIA , Venezuela

   TO RECIFE , Brazil

      TO OAXACA , Mexico

         TO SAO PALO , Brazil

✓ TO CARACAS , Venezuela

✓ TO MANAGUA , Nicaragua

   ⌣ TO SAN SALVADOR , El Salvador

      ✓ TO PORT-AU-PRINCE , Haiti

         TO PORTO ALEGRE Brazil

         TO MONTEGO BAY, Jamaica

where they caught the culprit trying to sell the recipe.

I'LL STAY RIGHT HERE AND MAKE SURE THE ROBBER DOESN'T COME BACK FOR MORE NACHOS!

Nachos Nabbed

The Mystery:

HOW MANY DIFFERENT COUNTRIES DID THE OFFICERS VISIT DURING THEIR SEARCH?

16

Name_____

Suspicious Cargo

HMMM. . . GOLD BRICKS, TOO HEAVY FOR A PLANE?. . . FRAGILE CREAM PUFFS?. . . LIVE PIRHANNAS IN TANKS?. . . STOLEN PEPPERONI?. . . A RARE RHINOSCEROS?. . . A MILLION MEATBALLS?

Rosco is sharing a ride with a friend. But his friend is mysterious about the cargo in the truck. He tells Rosco that this load cannot be put on an airplane, and that he will be well paid to get it to the destination safely. Also, he has been asked to drive carefully, avoiding sudden stops and bumpy roads.

Although the mysterious cargo piques Rosco's curiosity, he is satisfied with the large supply of cheese his friend has provided. He hopes to find even more exotic cheeses in this interesting part of the world.

The truck is loaded in Saskatoon, Saskatchewan, Canada.
The final destination is Charlottetown, Prince Edward Island, Canada.

The Mysteries:

CAN THE TRIP ACTUALLY BE MADE BY TRUCK (ON LAND OR BRIDGES, WITH NO NEED FOR FERRIES OR OTHER BOATS)?

WHAT DO YOU SUSPECT IS IN THE TRUCK?   WHAT LEADS YOU TO THIS SUSPICION?

Name_____

The Abducted Scientist

Geologist Dr. Carlotta Gold has been abducted. Her secret research led to the location of a gold vein—one of the largest ever discovered. But the word got out. She has been captured and taken somewhere deep in Africa. Rosco just happens to be in the area. The curious rat is on his way to explore the capital city of Khartoum.

Rosco's plane has just taken off from the capital city of Dakar. It is headed due east along the same line of latitude as Dakar. When a tip comes in about Dr. Gold's location, his plane is diverted for a rescue attempt.

The message Rosco has received is this:

Dr. Gold's location:

Stay on the same course until you are directly south of Khartoum. She has been sighted on the banks of the last major river you will cross before turning north to Khartoum.

Proceed with caution. Her captors are unsavory characters.

The Mystery:

WHAT IS THE RIVER THAT THE RESCUERS NEED TO FIND?

Name_____

Caught on Camera

The camera is always clicking when Rosco travels. (He fancies himself an ace photographer!) Right now, he is traveling in Asia with some of his friends. All the pictures in his camera are from this picturesque area of the world.

ANOTHER PRIZE WINNER!

The Mystery:

WHICH OF THESE PICTURES COULD BE IN HIS CAMERA?

1. Meatball diving into the deepest, coldest lake in the world

2. Boomerang riding an elephant in a country where the elephant is a national symbol

3. Boomerang with a turtle in the Galapagos Islands

4. a boatload of tourists looking for the Loch Ness Monster

5. Portia meeting a Siberian tiger

6. a shot looking up at the world's highest waterfall

7. scenes from six different countries that end with the letters "stan"

8. Meatball wrestling a crocodile on the banks of the world's longest river

9. Portia paddling a canoe in a fjord

10. Rosco making friends with a Bengali tiger

Draw one of the pictures from Rosco's camera.

Name_____

Jungle Secrets

Jungles hold secrets. The deep, thick rainforests are natural places for someone to stash stolen diamonds, hide a runaway robber, or bury bags of silver. You might find rebel hideouts, exiled dictators, people escaping from angry relatives or creditors, partners plotting devious deeds, or just folks who have private dealings they don't want to share.

Rosco is off to a few of the world's jungles to snoop into some such secrets. It is uncanny how rats can wiggle their way into the most clandestine situations.

His travels take him to each of the countries listed. Not all the stops are in jungles. Sometimes the lure of exotic fish, cheese enchiladas, steamy peanut stew, or fresh banana pudding call for a diversion from the trip plan.

I CAN'T SEE A RESTAURANT FROM HERE!

Stop # 1:   Belize
Stop # 2:   Venezuela
Stop # 3:   Congo
Stop # 4:   Burma
Stop # 5:   South Africa
Stop # 6:   Argentina
Stop # 7:   El Salvador
Stop # 8:   Costa Rica
Stop # 9:   Mexico
Stop # 10: Honduras

Stop # 11: Thailand
Stop # 12: Brazil
Stop # 13: India
Stop # 14: Madagascar
Stop # 15: Australia
Stop # 16: Algeria
Stop # 17: Peru
Stop # 18: Malaysia
Stop # 19: Greece
Stop # 20: Liberia

The Mystery:

WHICH OF THE STOPS ARE IN COUNTRIES THAT ARE *NOT* HOME TO A JUNGLE?

Name_____

20

The Priceless Guitar

This guitar was said to be priceless. That's because the owner would not sell it for any price. But, alas, the owner fell on hard times, and put the guitar up for auction in a European city.

Rosco, that musical rat, got a chance to play the guitar for the prospective buyers who came to the auction.

There were 15 bidders—each from one of the following European countries:

Austria   Belgium   Bulgaria
Finland   France   Greece
Hungary   Ireland   Kosovo   Lithuania
Monaco   Montenegro   Portugal
Sweden   United Kingdom

The guitar sold for $2.3 million euros.

The Mysteries:

WHICH BUYERS WOULD HAVE TO CONVERT FROM THEIR HOME CURRENCY IN ORDER TO BUY THE GUITAR?

HOW MUCH WOULD THAT GUITAR COST (TODAY) IN AMERICAN DOLLARS?

HOW MUCH WOULD THAT GUITAR COST (TODAY) IN UK CURRENCY (THE POUND)?

Name_____

A Curious Message

Rosco, snoozing on a beach, sits up and takes notice when a bottle washes ashore. He wakes up even more when he reads the note in the bottle.

From the curious message in the bottle, Rosco infers that the writer is someone stranded on an island somewhere in the world.

He starts listing islands he can remember from his travels:

U.S. Virgin Islands   Fiji

Marshall Islands   Guam

Falkland Islands   Iceland

Aleutian Islands   Sardinia

Japanese Islands   Borneo

Philippines   Cuba

Madagascar   Jamaica

Pago Pago   Crete

Greenland   Sri Lanka

The Mystery:

WHICH OF THE ISLANDS ON ROSCO'S LIST IS MOST LIKELY TO BE NEAR THE LOCATION OF THE MAROONED WRITER?

Name_____

Close to Home

While visiting in Indiana, Rosco and a few friends decide to take a sightseeing trip by car. They know that Portia Mouse would like to drive no more than 1000 miles each way from their central Indiana location, so Rosco starts looking up attractions and landmarks that might be within that distance. Then he shifts his energies to packing up a food supply for the diverse appetites in the car.

ARE WE THERE YET?

Here's Rosco's list of some U.S. tourist attractions:

- Anasazi Indian Cliff Dwellings
- Rock and Roll Hall of Fame
- Everglades National Park
- Niagara Falls
- Carlsbad Caverns
- Gateway Arch
- The Alamo
- Mt. Rushmore
- Old Faithful Geyser
- Baseball Hall of Fame
- Mammoth Cave
- Death Valley

The Mystery:

HOW MANY OF THE LOCATIONS ON ROSCO'S LIST ARE *NOT* REALISTIC POSSIBILITIES FOR THIS TRIP?

Name_____

Trekking to Treasure

Recently-discovered maps of the Treasure Islands have an X marked at the highest point on each island. Does this mean there is treasure buried on every island? Rosco is a treasure hunter who wants to find out. So he sails to each island, grabs his shovel, and treks to the highest spot. After the search, he hikes back down to the boat (with or without treasure).

IT'S A LONG WAY UP, BUT I THINK IT'S GOING TO BE WORTH IT.

The Mystery:

HOW FAR (IN VERTICAL DISTANCE UP AND DOWN) DOES ROSCO TREK?

Elevation Key

sea level

each line ———
represents
a rise of
500 feet

Shipwreck Island

Doubloon Island

Cutlass Straight

Crow's Nest Island

Buccaneer Island

Smuggler's Cove

Spyglass Channel

Pirates Cove

Treasure Islands

N
W — E
S

Name_____

24

The Unasked Question

In the final round of a geography bee, judges submitted questions about physical geographic features. Rosco got all the answers correct. When the bee was over and the prize had been awarded, it was discovered that one judge's question had not been asked. Rosco agreed to answer that last question—just to prove his geography expertise. His answer was right!

The Geography Bee Questions

1. What is a fumarole?

2. Where is an alluvial deposit found?

3. What process is named by the word "orogeny"?

4. If you were lost in a savanna, where would you be?

5. What mixes with fog to form smog?

6. When you explore an erg, what is beneath your feet?

7. Where would you find the antipode to your current location?

8. If you're caught in a cataract, where are you?

9. What does a river meet at a confluence?

10. What carries loess?

11. ?????

A VOLCANIC CRACK IN THE GROUND

MOUNTAIN BUILDING

IN A SERIES OF WATERFALLS

WIND

SMOKE

AT PRECISELY THE OPPOSITE POINT ON EARTH

THE APHELION

A RIVER

AT THE FOOT OF A MOUNTAIN

IN A TROPICAL GRASSLAND

SAND

The Mystery: WHAT WAS THE UNASKED QUESTION?

Name_____

Geography Mysteries—Learning Adventures Series

Stranded in the Strait

It's amazing how many straits connect bodies of water in this world! Rosco is determined to explore all of them. One strait seems to capture him—literally. The current keeps him from moving forward. An abandoned freighter blocks the exit behind him.

He is stranded!

> HOW DO I GET OUT OF THIS STRAIT-JACKET?

The Mystery:

WHERE IS ROSCO?

- ✓ Strait of Gibraltar 非,西班牙
- Straits of Mackinac Michigan
- ✓ Bass Strait New Zelan
- ✓ Straits of Florida
- Strait of Sicily 突尼斯
- ✓ Cook Strait
- ✓ Strait of Malacca
- Hecate Strait 加拿大
- ✓ Strait of Magellan
- La Perouse Strait 日俄
- ✓ Strait of Hormuz 波斯湾

After two days, the cheese is gone (a disaster for Rosco). He radios for help, but his message is not clear.

The rescue team only gets these scattered bits of information as to Rosco's whereabouts:

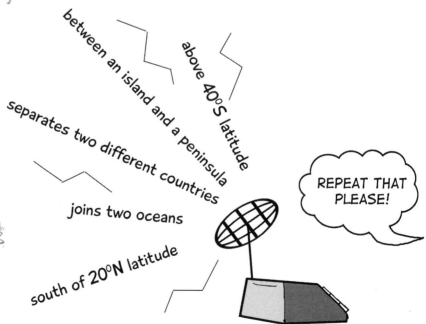

between an island and a peninsula

above 40°S latitude

separates two different countries

joins two oceans

south of 20°N latitude

> REPEAT THAT PLEASE!

Name_____

Emergency Delivery

MUSH!

THEY DON'T CALL ME THE CAN-DO KID FOR NOTHING!

A salmon cannery in Selawik, Alaska is out of cans! The whole season's catch of fresh salmon is in danger of going to waste. It will take a hearty dog team to get to seven locations around the state to pick up cans and deliver them to the cannery before that fish is unusable.

Rosco takes off from Yukutat, Alaska, with a fresh team of dogs and one thing on his mind: the salmon mousse on cheese crackers that is waiting for him at the end of the trip.

He stops in these towns (in this order) to pick up cans: Tok, Good News Bay, Holy Cross, Rampart, Chicken, Coldfoot, and Dead Horse. The last leg of the trip is from Dead Horse to Selawik.

The Mysteries:

WHICH OF THESE SEQUENCES OF DIRECTIONS IS RIGHT FOR ROSCO TO FOLLOW ON THIS TRIP?

1. NW, SW, NE, NE, SE, N, NE, S

2. NW, NW, E, NE, E, W, NE, SW

3. W, N, NE, NE, SE, NW, NE, SW

4. NW, SW, NE, NE, SE, NW, NE, S

5. NW, SW, NE, NE, SE, NW, NE, SW

WILL ROSCO CROSS THE YUKON RIVER ON HIS TRIP?

Name_____

The Missing Microchip

From his vacation spot in Mexico, Rosco hears the news: A microchip containing top secret codes has been stolen from NASA. It is thought that this will be sold to someone who intends to dangerously disrupt communications from dozens of satellites.

By some strange coincidence, the thieves have Rosco mixed up with the sinister buyer. Every day a bag of chips is delivered to his hotel room. A clue is written on one chip in the bag. When he puts all these clues together, Rosco will know where to pick up the microchip. But first, he must eat all the chips.

The Mystery:

WHERE IS THE MISSING MICROCHIP?

HEY, ARE THESE MACRO-CHIPS?

nacho Chips

#1 north of the equator

#2 capital city of a province

#3 11°30' E longitude

#5 once home to Leonardo da Vinci

#4 country that touches the Adriatic Sea

#6 building houses "The David" sculpture

#8 in a crack under the left little toe

#7 site of Ponte Vecchio over the Arno River

Name_____

The Elusive Recipe

THAT MEAL WAS FINGER-LICKING GOOD. I MUST HAVE THE RECIPE!

Portia Mouse went on vacation to Hawaii alone. Each time she attended a luau, she knew her friends had made a mistake to miss this trip. When she tasted the mouth-watering kalua pig served at a luau in Hilo, she decided she must get the recipe so she could cook some for Rosco and her friends when she got back home.

No one seemed to have the recipe. Portia flew from island to island following tips, without success. The night before she was to fly home from Lihue, she got the best lead: The recipe could be found in the back of a small grocery store in Hana. Portia took a chance. Early in the morning, she hired a helicopter and flew in a straight line from Lihue to Hana.

The Mystery:

WHICH OF THESE LAND AND WATER FEATURES DID PORTIA CROSS ON HER TRIP TO HANA?

Oahu 西北   a. Waianae Mountains
Oahu 东   b. Koolau Mountains
Hawaii   c. Mauna Loa
           d. Pearl Harbor
           e. Kauai Channel
           f. Kaiwi Channel
maui ◯   g. Pailolo Channel
Oahu 南   h. Mamala Bay

i. Island of Molokai
j. Island of Maui
k. Island of Hawaii
l. Island of Kauai
m. Island of Lanai
n. Island of Oahu
o. Waimea Canyon   Kauai 西
p. Wailuka River   Hawaii 东

Name_____

The Space Stowaway

During a tour of some USA tourist attractions, nosy Rosco wandered away from the crowd and found himself accidently locked inside a simulated space capsule. While he waited for help, he studied the view of Earth depicted on the screen inside. At that moment, the awesome image showed almost all of the northern, eastern, and southern hemispheres.

The Mysteries:

WHICH OF THE VIEWS ON THE RIGHT IS THE ONE THAT ROSCO SEES? (CIRCLE THE NUMBER.)

WHAT CONTINENT(S) DOES ROSCO *NOT* SEE IN THIS VIEW?

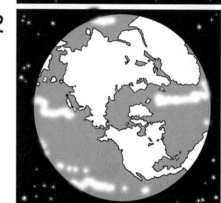

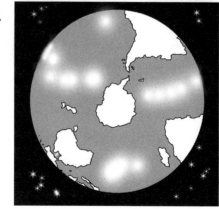

Name

Vanished at the Peak

Things have been disappearing on mountain-climbing expeditions. Shortly after parties reach the peak, some vital supply seems to vanish into thin air.

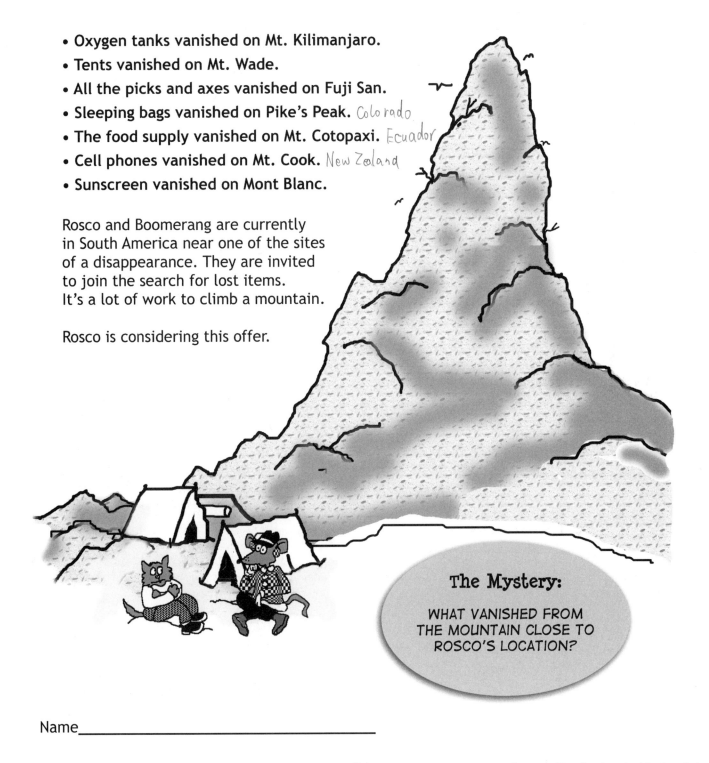

- Oxygen tanks vanished on Mt. Kilimanjaro.
- Tents vanished on Mt. Wade.
- All the picks and axes vanished on Fuji San.
- Sleeping bags vanished on Pike's Peak. Colorado
- The food supply vanished on Mt. Cotopaxi. Ecuador
- Cell phones vanished on Mt. Cook. New Zealand
- Sunscreen vanished on Mont Blanc.

Rosco and Boomerang are currently in South America near one of the sites of a disappearance. They are invited to join the search for lost items. It's a lot of work to climb a mountain.

Rosco is considering this offer.

The Mystery:

WHAT VANISHED FROM THE MOUNTAIN CLOSE TO ROSCO'S LOCATION?

Name_____

31

The Coffee Caper

FULL-BODIED, FRESH AROMA . . . BUT NOT QUITE THERE.

A highly-caffeinated crew of culprits concocted a clever coffee caper. They stole prize-winning gourmet coffee beans from the hills of Colombia and sold them for a very high price to a coffee dealer somewhere in Europe.

Rosco, who only drinks the **best** coffee, agrees to taste-test drinks in cafés throughout Europe. He is sure that he can identify a prize-winning coffee when he tastes it!

He drinks coffee in these cities:

阿尔巴尼亚 Latvia   爱尔兰

Tirane, Riga, Dublin,

法 **Marseilles, Amsterdam,** 荷 croatia

英 **Manchester, Valencia, Zagreb,**

保加利亚 **Sofia, Naples, Tartu,** Estonia

Ukraine **Odessa, Lisbon** 葡萄牙

Italy   spain

Rosco tracks the smuggled coffee to a tiny café down a quiet side street in a city northeast of Istanbul. He gathers enough evidence to provide the police with grounds for a search. Indeed, they raid the adjoining coffee-roasting business and find the beans!

The Mystery:

IN WHAT COUNTRY DOES ROSCO FIND THE STOLEN BEANS?

Name_____

Suspects on the Slopes

While skiers enjoy the powdery slopes, six sneaky thieves rob the Summit Lodge. One packs the money and they all ski away. They are all dressed alike to confuse anyone who might try to catch up with the cash.

Unfortunately for the crooks, Rosco witnesses the robbery, noticing that the skier with the money is the one who just finished a tuna sandwich at the restaurant.

Rosco follows the scent down Stomach Drop Hill, cuts under the lift to Broken Trail, skis to the intersection of Broken Trail and Big Bump Run, cuts straight over to Demon Run, above Half Way Hut to the junction of Loony Loop and Treacherous Trail. There the scent of tuna fish becomes overpowering as a skier runs right into Rosco.

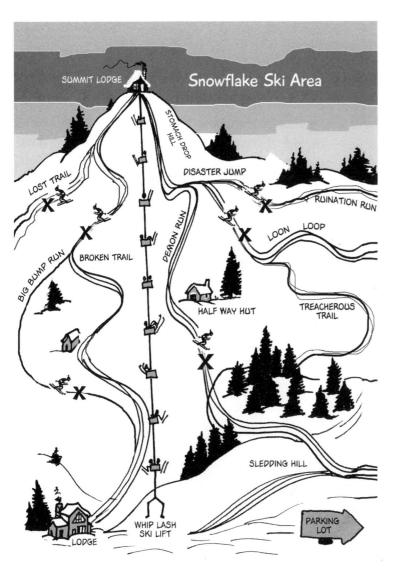

Snowflake Ski Area

SUMMIT LODGE

STOMACH DROP HILL

DISASTER JUMP

LOST TRAIL

RUINATION RUN

DEMON RUN

LOON LOOP

BIG BUMP RUN

BROKEN TRAIL

HALF WAY HUT

TREACHEROUS TRAIL

SLEDDING HILL

WHIP LASH SKI LIFT

LODGE

PARKING LOT

The Mystery:

WHICH SKIER SUSPECT HAS THE CASH? (CIRCLE THE SUSPECT. FIND ALL SUSPECTS BY THE X'S.)

Name_____

Cave Ciphers

When Rosco hears about the coded message rumored to be written on some cave walls, he gets into his spelunking attire and joins the search. That's because the message reveals the secret location of some buried treasure—a chest full of the rarest caviar.

I'VE NEVER TASTED CAVIAR, BUT I LIKE THE SOUND OF IT.

Each of the first four caves he visits holds a coded word. The final three caves hold the cipher (clues to break the code). He writes the coded words in order, then uses the cipher to substitute letters. This gives him the location of the last cave—where the chest is buried.

CIPHERS FROM THE CAVE WALLS

Pandalin Cave, Myanmar	ODGV
Dragon's Lair, Poland	MXSVE
Eistiesenwelt Ice Cave, Austria	TC
Mammoth Cave, Kentucky, USA	STDFRVE
Sarawak Chamber, Borneo	T = O, R = M, F = I, M = C
Lascaux Cave, France	X = A, S = V, O = B, C = F
Cango Cave, South Africa	V = E, D = L, G = U, E = S

The Mystery:

IN WHAT LOCATION (AND WHAT COUNTRY) WILL HE FIND THE CAVIAR?

Name_____

The Recovered Hockey Puck

A scheming thief embedded a precious black diamond in a hockey puck, then shipped dozens of pucks to hockey rinks and teams across Canada. His (or her) hope was to throw authorities off the track of the real diamond.

To catch this clever thief, Rosco enlists the help of his friend Meatball—an experienced hockey player. With his hockey skills, it is easy for Meatball to get invited to play games in all the places the diamond is suspected to be. (He must hit that puck in order to feel the presence of the diamond.) So he plays hockey in dozens of Canadian towns—on the border of Alaska, in the Rocky Mountains, along Hudson Bay, along the shores of Lake Superior, and all the way to Nova Scotia and Newfoundland.

One frigid night, Meatball plays at a rink on an island in a province bordering the Northwest Territory, Manitoba, and the Hudson Strait.

He hits a puck that has a different weight, and he knows he has found the one that holds the diamond.

The Mystery:

IN WHAT CANADIAN PROVINCE DID MEATBALL RECOVER THE HOCKEY PUCK?

Name_____

Arachnid Encounter

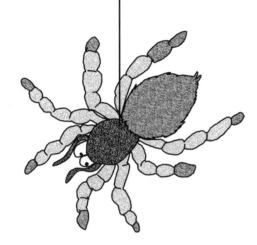

Rosco's travels take him to a place he has never been—a place that is home to the largest spider in the world.

Most visitors shudder at the tales of this arachnid, and Rosco isn't eager to encounter one. But if he does, he swears he won't be intimidated by a common spider.

(No one told him that the Goliath Birdeater tarantula can grow to be one foot long!)

The Mystery:

IN WHAT AREA OF THE WORLD WOULD ROSCO BE WHEN HE MEETS GOLIATH?

GET ME OUT OF HERE!

Name_____

36

Separated on the Serengeti

ROSCO!

Boomerang thinks Serengeti sounds a lot like "spaghetti" so he's hoping to find some food out here. He's so focused on his stomach that he wanders away from the guide and the truck and loses track of where he is going. What's worse: He gets separated from his safari partner, Rosco.

The Mystery:

WHILE BOOMERANG AND ROSCO ARE WANDERING THE SERENGETI LOOKING FOR EACH OTHER, WHICH OF THESE THINGS ARE THEY *NOT* LIKELY TO ENCOUNTER?

- roaming zebras
- the largest overland migration of animals
- game reserves
- grasslands
- roving grizzly bears
- the Mara River
- national parks
- year-round rainfall
- a border between two countries
- herds of wildebeasts
- roaming antelopes

BOOMERANG?

Name_____

The Botched Train Robbery

When the Diesel brothers planned to rob a train, they got creative. They decided to lead a herd of cattle onto the train tracks, stop the train, heist the safe full of gold, and cart it away on super-charged trucks. In addition, they thought it would be cool to do this at the site of a famous train robbery from the past. So they chose one of these historic robberies:

- **The Great Train Robbery (1963)**
- **The Bezdany Raid (1908)**
- **The Wilcox Train Robbery (1899)**
- **The Kakori Train Robbery (1925)**
- **The Great Gold Robbery of 1855**

Their plan may have been inventive, but it was far from clever or careful. Somehow, one of the brothers (Doyle) ended up locked inside the safe while the cows stormed onto the train, injuring the other thieves.

On that very day, quite by coincidence, Rosco was visiting a town close to the site of the botched train robbery. He was at a train museum, satisfying his curiosity about the history of the long-ago robbery. This museum was located at 54°54′N, 23°56′E. He heard the news and got to the site just in time to see the culprits apprehended and sent off to the hoosegow by rail.

IT SOUNDS LIKE A FUTURE EXHIBIT IN THE HISTORIC TRAIN MUSEUM TO ME!

Train robbery Botched by Dumb Robbers

The Mystery:

WHICH ONE OF THE HISTORIC TRAIN ROBBERIES TOOK PLACE NEAR THE SITE OF THIS BOTCHED ATTEMPT?

DOYLE DID IT AGAIN!

Name_____

Imminent Eruptions

When Rosco goes to visit sites around the Ring of Fire, he's expecting to see fantastic circus acts with big cats leaping through burning rings. (Didn't he read the travel brochure?)

Instead, he stumbles into volcano territory. Everywhere he goes, things are rumbling and eruptions are imminent. On this particular day, he gets much too close to the mountain, and an eruption sends him running for his life.

The Mystery:

WHICH OF THESE MOUNTAINS COULD **NOT** BE THE ONE THAT'S ERUPTING DURING ROSCO'S TRIP TO THE RING OF FIRE?

- Mt. Pinatubo, Philippines
- El Chichon, Mexico
- Mt. St. Helens, Oregon, USA
- Mt. Bandai, Japan
- Mt. Lassen, California, USA
- Mt. Kamen, Russia
- Mt. Ruapehu, New Zealand
- Mt. Llaima, Chile
- Mt. Erebus, Antarctica
- Mt. Etna, Italy
- Mt. Askja, Iceland
- Mt. Kratakau, Indonesia
- Kilauea, Hawaii, USA
- Mt. Sishaldin, Aleutian Islands

YIKES, A RAT COULD REALLY GET A HOT FOOT AROUND HERE!

Name_____

Rat Overboard

Rosco is fascinated to hear that the world is full of capes. He sets off to explore them.

He sails around these ten capes:

Cape of Good Hope 非
Cape Horn 南美
Cape San Antonio 古巴
Cape Comorin 印
Cape Matapan 希
Cape Wrath 英
Cape Roca
Cape Dezhnev 俄
Cape Cod 美
Cape Morris Jesup

On one of the voyages, Rosco hovers too close to the bow of the ship and is washed overboard by a powerful wave. Luckily, his mate scoops him out of the water, and hangs him up to dry.

THAT WAS A CLOSE ES-CAPE!

IT LOOKS AS IF ROSCO WILL BE HANGING AROUND THE BOAT TODAY.

The Mystery:

WHICH OF THESE BODIES OF WATER COULD *NOT* BE THE ONE FROM WHICH ROSCO IS RESCUED?

Indian Ocean
Atlantic Ocean
Mediterranean Sea
Pacific Ocean
Arabian Sea
Tasman Sea
Caribbean Sea
Bering Straits

Name_____

40

A Broken Promise

When Rosco went off to search for the tastiest cheesecake in the United States, he assured friends Boomerang, Portia, and Meatball that they could join him when he located the best ones. He never called. Instead, he lingered a while in each of five states that had "to-die-for" cheesecake. Use the clues and the shapes to identify these states.

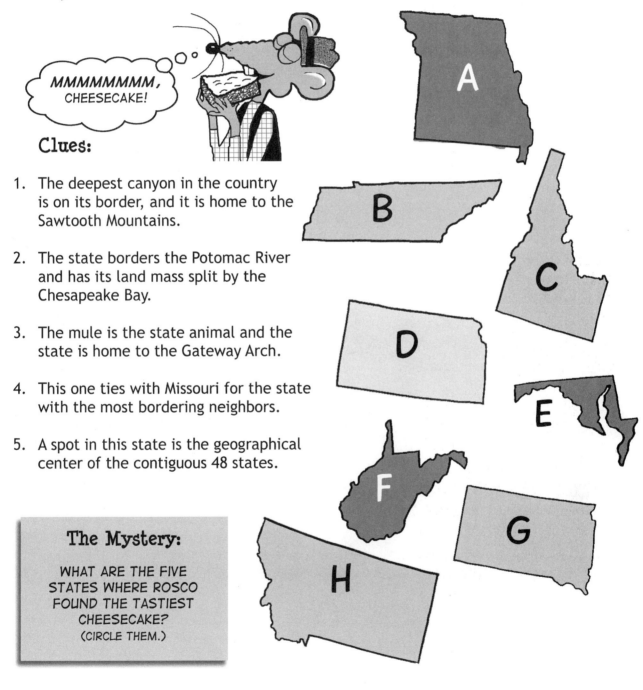

MMMMMMMM, CHEESECAKE!

Clues:

1. The deepest canyon in the country is on its border, and it is home to the Sawtooth Mountains.

2. The state borders the Potomac River and has its land mass split by the Chesapeake Bay.

3. The mule is the state animal and the state is home to the Gateway Arch.

4. This one ties with Missouri for the state with the most bordering neighbors.

5. A spot in this state is the geographical center of the contiguous 48 states.

The Mystery:

WHAT ARE THE FIVE STATES WHERE ROSCO FOUND THE TASTIEST CHEESECAKE? (CIRCLE THEM.)

Name_____

Run Aground in the Archipelago

What luck! Each time Rosco visits an archipelago, some ship bearing a large load of food runs aground, spilling its cargo. Rosco usually offers to help with the recovery, especially if it involves cheese.

He has recovered:

- tons of canned cheddar soup in Tierra del Fuego

- a shipment of cheese fondue in the Bahamas

- a thousand jars of Alfredo Parmesan sauce in the Aegean Islands

- a boatload of cheese sausages in the Solomon Islands

- a batch of frozen four-cheese pizzas in the Aleutians

SOGGY CHIPS! WHAT A TRAGEDY!

The Mysteries:

WHERE HAS GARFIELD BEEN WHEN HE HAS RECOVERED THESE ITEMS? (DESCRIBE THE LOCATIONS.)

WHY MIGHT A SHIP RUN AGROUND IN OR NEAR AN ARCHIPELAGO?

Name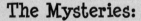

Follow the Torch

Rosco manages to get invited to join the exclusive group of
Olympic torchbearers. He carries the torch for a section of
the European route (and stops often for the energizing snacks).

During this month, the torch is transported on foot and by truck

from Lisbon, Portugal

to Bern, Switzerland

to Budapest, Hungary

to Sofia, Bulgaria

to Minsk, Belarus

to Tashkent, Uzbekistan.

The torch travels by as direct
a route as possible between cities.

The Mystery:

THROUGH HOW MANY OF THESE COUNTRIES IS
THE TORCH LIKELY TO PASS ON ITS JOURNEY?

Portugal	Croatia	Bulgaria	Russia
Belarus	Romania	Lithuania	Austria
Uzbekistan	Ukraine	Kazakhstan	Serbia
Spain	France	Turkmenistan	Poland
Switzerland	Hungary	Belgium	Slovakia

Name_____

The Au Gratin Sleuth

Rosco visits several foreign countries to see amazing human-built attractions. His first stop is always at an eatery to try out the local potatoes au gratin (or whatever dish is closest to it).

On this trip, Rosco's favorite dish and favorite attraction are found in the same country. This is the country (of all those he visits) that has the greatest number of neighbors (countries that border it).

He visits these attractions:

I THINK I'M GOING TO NEED AN ORDER TO GO!

- the Sphinx
- the Panama Canal
- Buckingham Palace
- Prague Castle
- Taj Mahal
- Persepolis
- Chichen Itza Ruins
- Palace of Versailles

(sampled potatoes au gratin in each location!)

The Mystery:

WHICH OF THESE ATTRACTIONS IS ROSCO'S FAVORITE?

Name_____

A Noodle in a Haystack

An unusually clever jewel thief posed as a waiter in an exclusive Italian restaurant. When the power went out temporarily, she lifted a priceless pearl necklace from a wealthy diner, broke the string, and stuffed the pearls inside a tube of cheese manicotti (which is a large hollow noodle)!

Then, this crafty crook took off in a small plane and dropped the noodle over a hayfield. She intended to retrieve the pearls when it was safe to do so.

I DREAMT THAT A NOODLE FELL FROM THE SKY, AND I ATE IT!

Her plan was perfect—except for the rat. This waiter-thief-pilot did not know that Rosco would be napping on the other side of that haystack.

The thief did return to this dairy farm in a remote area near the southern end of the Gulf of Riga. But by then, the noodle had been eaten and the pearls had been turned over to the police.

The Mystery:

WHERE IN THE WORLD IS THAT HAYSTACK?

Name_____

The Frozen Message

Rats have a way of picking up secrets. That's because they spend a lot of time trying to be as inconspicuous as possible. That is the case today. Rosco overhears a group of shady characters bragging about their success in a holdup. They review their plans for stashing the cash in a remote location.

Rosco heads for the police station to share the secret. The trouble is, a big wind blows him into a snow drift and he just about freezes before he gets there. He needs time to thaw out before he can pass along the message he's got memorized.

As he thaws, Rosco is able to give these clues he overheard:

through the Strait of Magellan

across the Drake Passage

at the base of Mt. Rex

The Mystery:

WHERE ARE THE ROBBERS PLANNING TO HIDE THE MONEY?

Name_____

The Melted Clues

Rosco and Boomerang are on an adventure along the equator when they hear that poachers have captured an endangered member of a cat species. Boomerang just can't ignore the plight of a fellow cat.

Many items are found at the site where the poachers waited to capture the cat. But no fingerprints are left because all the clues have melted in the intense heat: the chocolate bars, water jugs, plastic bags, packages of cheese, and containers of peanut butter.

It's a good thing Boomerang is along, because a cat can sniff out another cat the way no human can. After sniffing at the melted chocolate bars, cheese, and peanut butter, he picks up the scent and leads the search.

I'M *HOT* ON THE TRAIL.

PANT

PANT

The Mystery:

WHICH OF THESE COULD BE THE COUNTRY WHERE ROSCO AND BOOMERANG ARE SEARCHING?

Tuvalu	Liberia
Indonesia	Kenya
Maldives	Colombia
Papua New Guinea	Equatorial Guinea
Gabon	Ecuador
Somalia	Uganda
Kiribati	

Name_____

The Last Phone Call

Exhausted from his travels, Rosco decides to pursue the world's great cheese dishes right from the comfort of his home—by using the phone.

He consults the Internet to make a list of numbers for restaurants around the world. He wants to find out if the food is promising enough to warrant a tasting trip. Rosco believes that he can get the best information about dishes by talking directly to the cooks.

Around noon on Monday (Rosco's home time, USA Eastern Standard Time), he places six calls. He gets answering machines, and leaves messages. All the cooks return his calls. The last call is the one that interests him most.

Return calls
(Time is local for each city.)

Malolos, Philippines	at 6:20 AM Tues
Kehei, Hawaii	at 7:15 PM Mon
Timaru, New Zealand	at 7 AM Tues
Mercedes, Uruguay	at 6 PM Mon
Toliora, Madagascar	at 8 AM Tues
Santa Ana, El Salvador	at 5:30 PM Mon

The Mystery:

FROM WHAT LOCATION IS THE LAST CALL AND AT WHAT TIME DOES ROSCO RECEIVE IT?

Name_____

The Misplaced Mummies

Something is wrong in Giza Square. Mummies are missing. The authorities are always alert for culprits trying to steal mummies, so they cannot have been removed from the square. But clearly, mummies of two queens, two nobles, and one of the royal children are not where they belong.

Clues have been left behind—clues which seem to indicate that the mummies are still in the area:

The Mystery:

WHERE ARE THE MUMMIES?
(CIRCLE THE LOCATIONS.)

- BENEATH ROYAL BARGE, SOUTHEAST CORNER OF KHUFU'S TOMB
- BESIDE THE NOBLE'S TOMB FARTHEST WEST OF THE SPHINX
- BEHIND EASTERNMOST MENKAURE'S QUEEN TOMB
- BEHIND FARTHEST WEST CHILD'S TOMB
- BEHIND VALLEY TEMPLE EAST OF KHAFRE'S QUEEN

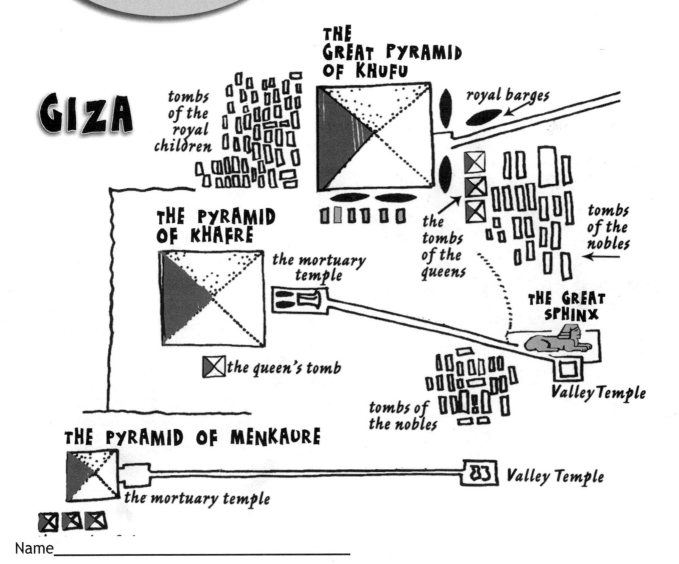

Name_____

49

The Post-it® Bandit

Rosco researches and plans carefully for his upcoming trip to the Eastern Hemisphere. He uses Post-it® notes to mark the map on his bulletin board with the attractions he wants to see:

SB — St. Basil's Cathedral
ET — Eiffel Tower
GW — Great Wall of China
P-S — Pyramids and Sphinx
P — Parthenon
S — Stonehenge
LT — Leaning Tower of Pisa
TM — Taj Mahal

His plans are foiled when someone sneaks in during his nap, steals two notes, replaces them with blanks, and rearranges some of his carefully-placed notes on the board.

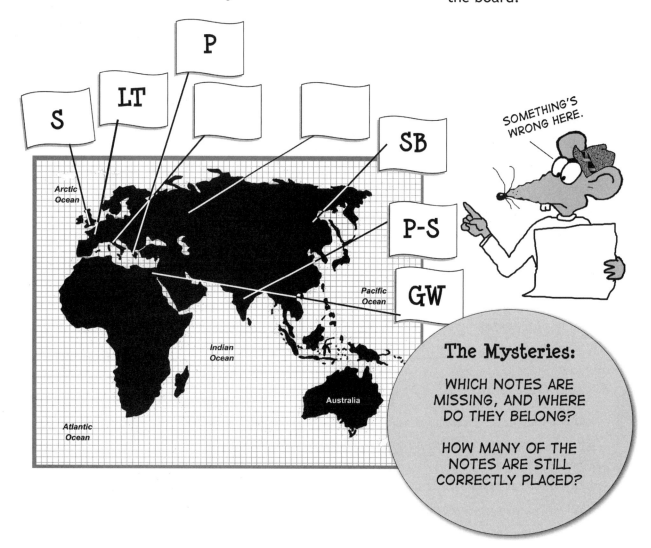

SOMETHING'S WRONG HERE.

The Mysteries:

WHICH NOTES ARE MISSING, AND WHERE DO THEY BELONG?

HOW MANY OF THE NOTES ARE STILL CORRECTLY PLACED?

Name_____

A Furious Chase

When a quick-fingered tourist snatches Rosco's cell phone in Luxembourg, the spunky rat is not about to let her get away. After all, that phone has the numbers of the most important cheese producers in the world!

Rosco hops on his motorbike in hot pursuit of the thief. To retrieve that phone, he rides several days and travels (by land or boat):

SCOUNDREL!

- over flat-topped hills,
- in and out of deep narrow valleys with steep sides,
- along coastlines that jut out into water,
- through dry sandy regions,
- over steep mounds of sand,
- along narrow strips of land that connect two larger bodies of land,
- along small rivers that flow into larger rivers, and
- around areas where rivers empty into lakes.

The Mystery:

WHICH OF THESE LANDFORMS OR WATER FORMS ARE *NOT* ENCOUNTERED IN HIS PURSUIT?

strait	tributary	dune
fjord	oasis	mouth
cape	mesa	desert
canyon	isthmus	gulf

Name_____

The Phony Alibi

Swiss chocolate is rumored to be the finest in the world, so as soon as he gets off the plane, Rosco heads straight to the nearest chocolate shop. He arrives on a Tuesday afternoon in July, just before the 6:00 PM closing time. In his rush, he bumps into a bundled-up customer just leaving.

Oh, no! Just moments before, the shop had been robbed. All the chocolates are gone, and Rosco may have witnessed the culprit!

By the next morning, the police are questioning a chocolate-covered suspect. Evidence consists of chocolate on clothing and chocolaty fingerprints at the scene.

Sadly, Rosco can't identify the suspect, and the man has an alibi from a friend in Perth, Australia.

Rosco reads the alibi, and assures the police that the friend's statement is a lie.

Alibi

Chester could not have robbed that shop. He was on the phone with me at exactly that time.
I remember that I was just feeding my kids an early breakfast when the call came at what would have been 5:30 to 6:30 PM in Switzerland.

School is out for summer vacation, and we were getting ready to go off and spend the day at the beach. Chester and I talked for an hour.

NOT A CHANCE!

The Mystery:

HOW DOES ROSCO KNOW THAT THE ALIBI IS PHONY?

Name_____

Trouble at the Hotel

Rosco and Boomerang are having some trouble checking into the hotel. After a long trip, both of them are interested in one thing: getting into a room and getting to sleep.

Their journey of many hours brings them to a country that:

- is farther west than the Philippines

- is farther east than India

- is farther north than Malaysia

- is farther south than Bhutan

- borders the Gulf of Thailand

- does not border the South China Sea

- does not border the Bay of Bengal

The Mystery:

WHERE IN THE WORLD IS THIS HOTEL?

Name_____

The Undelivered Post Cards

MONTY IN LONDON . . .
MONIKA IN SARAJEVO . . .
ALI IN KUWAIT CITY . . .

I HOPE I DON'T
FORGET ANYONE!

List of Post Cards Sent

1. England
2. Bosnia
3. Kuwait
4. North Korea
5. Denmark
6. Oman
7. Borneo
8. Senegal
9. Trinidad and
   Tobago
10. Belize
11. Bangladesh
12. Mongolia
13. Grenada
14. Haiti
15. Suriname
16. New Caledonia

Rosco makes friends everywhere he goes. He keeps in touch with them by sending postcards to places as varied as

North and Central America,
South America,
Eastern Europe,
Western Europe,
Africa,
Northern Asia,
Middle East,
Southwestern Asia,
Southeast Asia,
and Oceania.

Unfortunately, every fourth post card on Rosco's list never reaches its destination. Fortunately, many gossipy replies (and pizza recipes) are sent back to him.

The Mystery:

HOW MANY OF THE WORLD'S REGIONS ARE *NOT* REACHED BY ONE OR MORE OF ROSCO'S POST CARDS?

Name_____

54

The Itinerary Mix-Up

Rosco is off to Scotland and the island of Ireland with his itineraries in hand. As usual, he has a made a list of things he wants to see and do in each location. But something is wrong with the lists!

in Ireland . . .

1. Eat Irish Stew in Belfast.

2. Visit Cape Clear.

3. Take pictures of Giant's Causeway.

4. Eat fruitcake in Glasgow.

5. Swim in St. George's Channel.

6. Eat pancakes in Londonderry.

7. Hunt for the Loch Ness Monster.

8. Sail on the North Sea.

9. See the dungeon at Blarney Castle.

10. Jet ski on Lough Neagh.

in Scotland . . .

1. Eat mashed potatoes in Dublin.

2. Sail to the Hebrides Islands.

3. Find pizza in Edinburgh.

4. Eat Scotch pies in Aberdeen.

5. Swim in Donegal Bay.

6. Drink coffee in the coffee shop where J. K. Rowling began writing the Harry Potter books.

7. Read limericks in the town of Limerick.

8. See the Firth of Fourth.

WELL, HERE'S ONE PROBLEM. I FORGOT TO LIST "EAT CHEESE SCONES."

The Mystery:

WHICH ITEMS ARE ON THE WRONG LIST?

Name_____

Pursuit of a Pizza Substitute

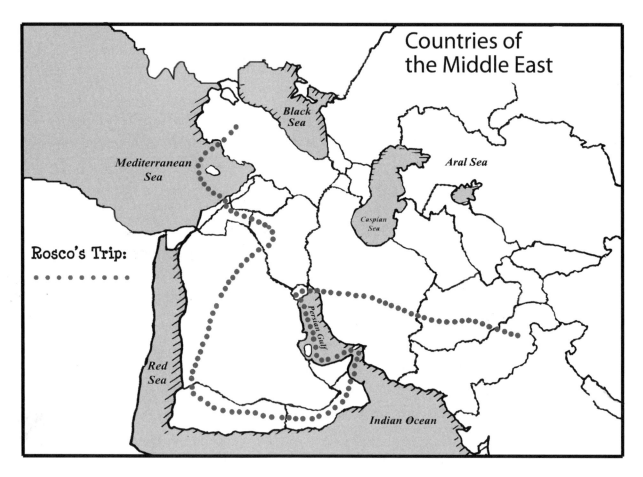

Countries of the Middle East

Black Sea

Mediterranean Sea

Aral Sea

Caspian Sea

Rosco's Trip:

. . . .

Persian Gulf

Red Sea

Indian Ocean

Pizza is no doubt a favorite food of Rosco's. He'll eat any kind anywhere. When he hears about the Middle Eastern flatbreads such as lavash and pita, he thinks they sound a lot like pizza dough.

Rosco makes a list of countries to visit, then follows his stomach—having a great time eating his way around the Middle East.

Rosco's list:

Afghanistan
Iran
Kuwait
Yemen
Saudi Arabia
Iraq
Israel

A LITTLE SAUCE, A LITTLE CHEESE, AND VOILA!

The Mystery:

WHAT COUNTRIES DOES ROSCO VISIT THAT ARE **NOT** ON HIS LIST?

Name_____

56

The Tough Question

It's geography bee season. Rosco finds himself, once again, in the semifinal round. This is one of the toughest questions he has had to answer in all his geography-bee experience.

Will Rosco still be in the bee when he's done with this question? Rosco has been to all of these countries. Did he pay as much attention to the geography as he did to the food?

The Question:

WHICH OF THESE COUNTRIES HAS THE GREATEST NUMBER OF NEIGHBORS SHARING A BORDER?

India

Guatemala

Botswana

Afghanistan

Macedonia

Romania

Cote D'Ivorie

Paraguay

Slovakia

Democratic Republic of the Congo

Bolivia

Iran

Rosco's Answer:

DEMOCRATIC REPUBLIC OF THE CONGO

The Mystery:

IS ROSCO'S ANSWER CORRECT?

Name_____

Extreme Conditions

A FORMULA LIKE THIS IS IRREPLACABLE!

Rosco is on the hunt again. This time it's a search for a stolen formula. Only the top scientists at the Rola Cola factory know how to make this best-selling drink. The formula is kept locked in a heavy vault except for those few moments each month when the scientists refresh their memories before mixing up a new batch. But now it is missing. The cola company owners must get it back before the thieves can figure out how to read and copy the electronic file.

This extreme emergency calls for extreme measures. Rosco tracks the thieves by GPS, and parachutes into locations where they might be found. The thieves make the chase more interesting (and challenging) by hiding out in locations with some of the world's most extreme conditions.

Rosco drops into countries (or other places) where these can be found:

1. the coldest temperature ever recorded
2. the hottest temperature ever recorded
3. the longest cave system in the world
4. the deepest cave in the world
5. the wettest spot in the world
6. the driest spot in the world
7. the longest fjord in the world
8. the windiest spot ever recorded

The Mystery:

INTO WHAT PLACES DOES ROSCO'S SEARCH TAKE HIM?

Name_____

The Uninvited Guest

Rosco is repeatedly surprised (and annoyed) by a pesky crab that joins in on his seashore vacation. This crab shows up everywhere he goes.

- When he explores the spit, the crab is right on his heels.

- When he crosses the lagoon, the crab scuttles behind.

- When he plays on the sandbar, the crab wants to play along.

- When he climbs on a stack, the crab is waiting for him.

- When he relaxes on the beach, the crab relaxes beside him.

- When he watches the sea life around a reef, the crab watches him.

- When he sails around an atoll, the crab is on the bow of the boat.

- When he surfs in the gulf, the crab clings to Rosco's surfboard.

The crab turns up in all his trip photos, except one: the one that includes a formation of resistant rock left standing after softer rock is worn away.

The Mystery:

WHAT SHORELINE FEATURE IS SHOWN IN THE PHOTO WITHOUT THE CRAB?

Name_____

The Backwards Mystery

Champ the Bobcat is the revered mascot of Montana State University. When his mascot uniform is stolen during a break-in at the athletic department, the entire state is up in arms.

To avoid being caught, the thief poses as a real bobcat and crisscrosses the U.S.A. on airplanes. His luck runs out when he steps off a plane in Lexington, Kentucky. He runs right into Rosco; and Rosco knows a phony cat when he sees one.

Eventually, authorities piece together the thief's escape route.

- The thief is apprehended in Kentucky at 8 PM on Friday as he gets off a flight that had left Alaska at 9 AM (Alaska time).

- Before the flight, he spent 10 hours in Alaska.

- He flew to Alaska from Hawaii, spending 4 hours in the air.

- Before that, he was in Hawaii for 2 hours.

- He left Arizona at noon (Arizona time) and flew 7 hours to Hawaii.

- He was in Arizona for 12 hours.

- He got to Arizona by traveling 6 hours from Virginia.

- He spent 2 hours in Virginia.

- Two hours after the theft was discovered, he left Montana for a 5-hour flight to Virginia.

CATCHING THE THIEF WAS ACADEMIC, REALLY. ALL IT TOOK WAS A GOOD TIME ZONE MAP, AND THE NOSE OF A RAT!

leave Montana
in Virginia
leave Virginia
in Arizona
leave Arizona

The Mysteries:

WHEN WAS THE THEFT DISCOVERED? (WRITE THE TIME AND DAY.)

WHEN DID THE THIEF ARRIVE IN ARIZONA (ARIZONA TIME AND DAY)?

Name_____

The Lure of the Islands

How can Boomerang possibly refuse Rosco's invitation to visit a place named the South Sandwich Islands? He can't! When he reads the add in Rosco's travel magazine, he's more determined than ever to get there as quickly as possible.

The Mystery:

WHICH OF THESE PROBABLY ARE *NOT* TRUE ABOUT BOOMERANG'S LOCATION?

1. He's in a small chain of eight islands.
2. The islands are owned by Great Britain.
3. He's just off the coast of Georgia, U.S.A.
4. The islands are bordered by the Atlantic Ocean.
5. He's just north of Cuba.
6. The islands have rugged mountains.
7. South America is the closest continent.
8. The islands are bordered by the Scotia Sea.
9. He's close to the equator.
10. There are dozens of sandwich shops on the islands.

Name_____

A Fortune in the Sand Trap

Rosco, an avid golfer, is enlisted to search for a stolen golf ball made of pure gold. Rumor has it that the thief fled to South America and actually played golf with the ball. But, being a lousy golfer, the crook soon lost the ball in a sand trap on a course somewhere on the continent.

Rosco takes two trips to South America to search, playing golf at these courses (in this order). Draw on the map his route for each trip. It may be helpful to use a different color pen for each route.

The Mystery:

ROSCO FINDS THE BALL IN THE COUNTRY WHERE HIS TWO ROUTES INTERSECT.

ON WHICH GOLF COURSE IS THE BALL STUCK IN THE SAND?

Trip 1
- CLUB PARAMARIBO IN PARAMARIBO, SURINAME
- MOKA GOLF COURSE IN MARAVAL, TRINIDAD
- EL RINCÓN GULF CLUB IN BOGATA, COLUMBIA
- LA PAZ GOLF COURSE IN LA PAZ, BOLIVIA
- QUITO TENNIS AND GOLF CLUB IN QUITO, ECUADOR
- LIMA GOLF COURSE IN LIMA, PERU

Trip 2
- CLUB DE GOLF LOS LEONES IN SANTIAGO, CHILE
- LAGUNITA COUNTRY CLUB IN BUENOS AIRES, ARGENTINA
- GOLF DEL CERRO IN MONTEVIDEO, URUGUAY
- PRAIA DO PAIVA IN RECIFE, BRAZIL
- CARLOS FRANCO COUNTRY CLUB IN ASUNCION, PARAGUAY
- VALLE ARRIBA GOLF COURSE IN CARACAS, VENEZUELA

Name_____

Fries Extraodinaire

Ahhhh! After many tries, Rosco finds what he believes to be the best French fries in the world. He returns often to this café in Southern France. One day he learns that the chef has been lured away to a job in another country. What's worse: there are differing reports as to the chef's new location.

Rosco follows all the leads, going to many cities and tasting fries as he goes. In four different cities, the fries are so close to perfection that he gives up his search for the chef. He decides instead to keep rotating among these places—eating the wonderful fries.

2 city farthest south on the tip of the Istria peninsula

1 city on the Pregolya River just upstream from Frisches Lagoon

3 town farthest southeast in the British Isles

4 city that lies in two European countries, split by the Danube River

CHOOSING THE BEST FRY IS GOING TO TAKE A LOT OF SAMPLING!

The Mystery:

WHAT ARE THE FOUR PLACES WHERE ROSCO GETS WAYLAID BY THE EXCELLENT FRIES?

Name_____

Geography Mysteries—Learning Adventures Series

The Grass Skirt Incident

Portia's hula lessons were so successful and impressive that she was invited to perform all over Polynesia.

In fact, her popularity sparked jealousy among some other dancers. Competition became so intense that someone switched the grass skirts backstage before a performance. This left Portia to perform in a skirt much too large for her. It's a good thing she came prepared for such a situation!

YOU WON'T CATCH ME OFF MY GUARD!

Portia performed on these islands:

New Zealand   Vanuatu   Line Islands   Elba
French Polynesia   Cook Islands   Phoenix Islands   Tonga
Barbados   Samoa   Christmas Island   Tuvalu
Pitcairn Islands   Channel Islands

The Mystery:

WHICH OF THE PERFORMANCE LOCATIONS COULD *NOT* BE THE PLACE WHERE THE GRASS SKIRT INCIDENT TOOK PLACE?

Name_____

64

Strange Stories

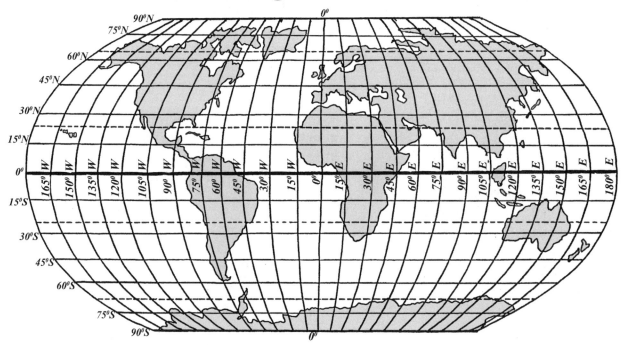

The job of a reporter is to get an unusual story—hopefully before anyone else gets it. Rosco's natural curiosity drives him to jet all over the world, finding out about strange events. As he does this, he counts the number of times he crosses key lines of latitude and longitude.

Here are the stories he investigates (in this order.) Letter(s) after each story show the direction(s) he travels to the next location.

The Stories

1) hundreds of enchiladas found wrapped in $100 bills in Guatemala (W & S)

2) baby gorilla lost in southern Gabon (N & E)

3) climbers held captive by Abominable Snowmen in the Himalayan Mountains of southern Tibet (W & S)

4) a two-year old who charms snakes on the southern tip of Argentina (W & N)

5) 80-foot popsicle in Northern Greenland (E & S)

6) lake once on fire in southern Finland

WOW! WHAT A STORY!

The Mystery:

HOW MANY TIMES DOES ROSCO CROSS EACH OF THESE AS HE TRAVELS TO GET THE SIX STORIES (STARTING IN THE COUNTRY OF THE FIRST STORY)?

____Arctic Circle   ____Antarctic Circle

____Tropic of Cancer   ____Tropic of Capricorn

____Equator   ____Prime Meridian

____International Date Line

Name_____

Imposters on Parade

Rosco loves a parade. He follows his favorite marching band as it tours the capital cities of several nations. But the good time is spoiled by crime when some imposters (who are also crooks) join the parade in one city.

Unbeknownst to Rosco and most of the band members, some thieves rent uniforms and join the band as a way of moving stolen musical instruments through the streets of the city without being noticed.

These are the capitals where the parades are held:

Wellington
Jakarta
Antananarivo
Buenos Aires
Mumbai
Maseru
Suva
Kuala Lumpur
Santiago
Colombo

One of these cities is the national capital that is farthest south in the world. The parade that is infiltrated by imposters takes place in another capital (listed above) closest in latitude to the southernmost capital.

The Mystery:

WHERE IS THE PARADE THAT
IS TROUBLED BY IMPOSTERS?
(CITY AND COUNTRY)

Name_____

The Bumpy Flights

I WONDER WHAT'S FOR LUNCH?

The travelers are already feeling cramped and grumpy from the long trip. Three stretches of heavy turbulence make them even more uncomfortable.

Each time, the pilot apologizes for the shaking and swaying of the plane, explaining that turbulence is common when flying over mountain ranges. This turbulence occurs when they have just left Mexico City heading east, and again after a stop in Rabat, Morocco, when they head east out over the Sahara Desert.

The third time they experience turbulence is when they cross from the European section of Russia into the Asian part of the country.

This time, the annoyance turns to excitement. The bumps and thumps shake open an overhead bin, and out spills a 20-gallon container of cheese balls. All of a sudden, Rosco becomes a fan of air turbulence.

The Mystery:

WHAT MOUNTAIN RANGES ARE THEY CROSSING WHEN THEY FEEL THE TURBULENCE EACH TIME?

Name_____

Million Dollar Fish

A group of jewel thieves escapes by boat after lifting millions of dollars worth of emeralds from a high-security museum in Venice. As they head out to sea, the Italian Guardia Costiera (coast guard) is suddenly on their tail. One thief panics and drops four of the jewels overboard. Floating down into the water, the shiny emeralds attract the attention of sea creatures—who swallow them up.

Since Boomerang is an expert on fish behavior, he helps out with the search. The Guardia Costiera hopes that Boomerangs's keen senses will lead him to the creatures with emeralds in their tummies.

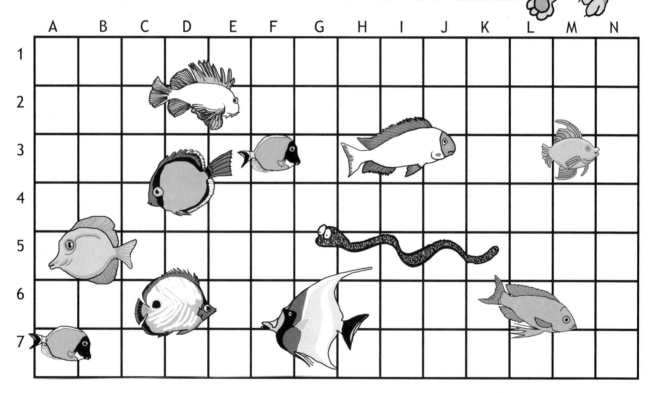

It doesn't take Boomerang long to solve the mystery. He identifies the creatures at these locations on the grid:

In F3   In G5, H5, I5, J5, K5

In A5 and B5   In L6 and M6

The Mystery:

WHICH CREATURES
SWALLOWED THE EMERALDS?
(CIRCLE THEM.)

Name_____

The Undercover Waiter

Rosco frequently goes undercover as a waiter at a fancy restaurant. This makes it easy for him to eavesdrop on conversations, pick up clues, follow suspects, and gather information on all sorts of mysteries. He has been to several places in this disguise:

- on an island where some people speak Papiamento
- in a country that has 14 sheep for every person
- in the largest city north of the Arctic Circle
- in a country that is home to the Aswan Dam
- in a city that used to be named Saigon
- in the smallest country in the world
- in every national capital located on the Danube River

IHR TISCH. . .

The Mystery:

WHERE HAS ROSCO BEEN (AS AN UNDERCOVER WAITER)?

Name_____

Purloined Provolone

There's excitement in the house when Rosco hears that seven groups of provolone fans around the world are competing to make the world's largest provolone.

There's horror in the house when Rosco learns that all seven of the record-breaking provolones have been stolen. Disappearing cheese is serious business to Rosco, and he's eager to help.

Rosco follows the distinctive scent and retrieves the missing record-breaking provolones in these locations:

- 35°S, 71°W

- 12°N, 85°W

- 7°N, 134°E

- 13°S, 17°E

- 53°N, 106°W

- 40°N, 59°E

- 5°S, 101°E

ONE DOWN, SIX TO GO!

The Mystery:

IN WHAT COUNTRIES DOES ROSCO FIND THE MISSING PROVOLONES?

Name_____

Intrigue in the Indies

While exploring the West Indies, Rosco gets caught up in the intrigue of piracy—and not the 18th-century history of pirates in the area. No, he's fascinated by the modern pirates with all the up-to-date technology.

News has it that a band of pirates has been circulating through the 2000-mile long chain of islands. They boldly rob food from yachts as the ships are docked for the night.

Reports of missing goods come in from

● Eleuthra

● Caicos

● eastern Cuba

● the Dominican Republic

● Puerto Rico

● Barbados

Authorities notice a pattern in the path of the pirates. Based on this, they make some assumptions about where the pirates will strike next.

The Mystery:

WHICH OF THESE ISLANDS IS LIKELY TO BE THE PIRATES' NEXT STOP: Jamaica, St. Croix, St. Lucia, Grand Cayman, or Haiti?

Name_____

Geo-Clues

It's a good thing she shares her friend Rosco's interest in geography, because Judge Portia needs it to decide these cases. She hears each accusation brought by the prosecution, listens to the defense, and makes a ruling.

NEXT CASE!

Judge Portia
presiding

CASE 1: Piracy in the Caribbean

Prosecution claims that Slick Sam chased down several ships with his fast yacht and robbed them during the week of September 4-10.

Defense insists Sam was not even using his boat during that time, because it had been damaged in a severe typhoon that struck off the coast of Cuba on September 3.

Ruling: for the prosecution

CASE 2: Penguin Poachers

Prosecution accuses Nadia and Inga of killing penguins in the Barents Sea off the coast of Arctic Russia.

Defense argues that the two friends have never been to the Barents Sea and have never harmed penguins or any other birds.

Ruling: for the defense

CASE 3: The Shifty Stargazer

Prosecution charges Lucy with stealing telescopes at a stargazing party in Costa Rica. Prosecutors say she lifted the goods while stargazers were awed by the colorful aurora borealis display.

Defense says Lucy was at the party, but did nothing other than enjoy the stars.

Ruling: for the defense

CASE 4: The Maquiladoras Alibi

Prosecution charges that Carlos passed forged checks to banks in his hometown of Malaga, Spain during the month of July.

Defense says Carlos was working during banking hours every day that month. His job, they say, is assembling coffee grinders at the local maquiladoras.

Ruling: for the prosecution

The Mystery: WHY DOES PORTIA CONFIDENTLY MAKE EACH OF THESE RULINGS?

Name_____

72

The Cover-Up

Soccer matches are notoriously rowdy, especially in parts of the world where soccer is the national obsession. Some gangs of clever pickpockets take advantage of this chaos. They synchronize their watches and lift wallets, jewelry, and other valuables at the same moment. Then they start fights throughout the stadium to cover up the thefts. This allows them to get away unnoticed.

As a part of the investigation, officials have arranged for Rosco to warm up with the players before several matches. This week, he's been on the home field with these teams:

- REAL MADRID (SPAIN)
- AL ORUBA (OMAN)
- ATLANTE (CANCUN, MEXICO)
- FC PORTO (PORTUGAL)
- OLYMPIAKOS (GREECE)
- KEYLANTAN (MALAYSIA)
- AGF (DENMARK)
- KALMAR FF (SWEDEN)
- AL AHLY CAIRO (EGYPT)

FIGHT!

POW! OW!

POW!

WHAM!

OOF!

The Mystery:

WHICH OF THESE PENINSULAS DOES ROSCO VISIT DURING THE INVESTIGATION?

- Indian
- Yucatan
- Balkan
- Malay
- Jutland
- Sinai
- Baja
- Scandinavian
- Korean
- Colaba
- Iberian
- Musandam

Name_____

Distress in the Desert

It's no surprise that Rosco decided to tour the world's largest deserts. He saw an article about these places, and thought it said: "Enjoy the marvels of the world's great **desserts**!"

Now here he is, distressed in the desert—looking for an oasis and seeing the occasional dessert mirage.

As promised, Rosco has seen some great deserts. Right now he is in a subtropical desert somewhere between **30⁰N latitude** and **30⁰S latitude**.

The Mystery:

WHICH OF THESE DESERTS COULD BE ROSCO'S CURRENT LOCATION?

- Mojave
- Sahara
- Atacama
- Namib
- Chihuahuan
- Kalahari
- Gobi
- Arabian
- Patagonia
- Great Sandy
- Arctic
- Iranian

Name_____

The Decoys

A thief with a sweet tooth planned a robbery with a clever escape. At a jellybean factory in San Francisco, she gathered up all the blueberry jellybeans into a huge bag. Then she hopped on a plane headed for southern California.

The Mystery:

WHERE DID ROSCO CATCH THE JELLYBEAN THIEF: ON THE SHORES OF THE MACKINAC STRAIT, ON THE SHORES OF LAKE OKEECHOBEE, OR ON THE SHORES OF THE DELAWARE BAY?

Over Eureka, she jumped out of a plane and landed in the sand dunes (where she had stashed a motorcycle). Two friends with motorcycles and large bags also waited in the dunes. She and the two decoys took off in different directions.

The thief took the route that crossed, passed, or followed these features: the Appalachian Mountains, the Coastal Mountains, the Sierra Nevada Range, Mt. Whitney, the Coastal Plains, the Central Valley, the Everglades, the Rio Grande River, and the Mojave Desert. Rosco caught up with her at the end of her route.

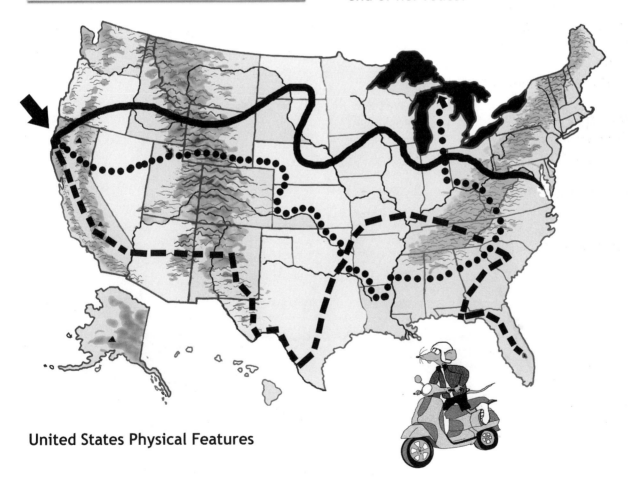

United States Physical Features

Name_____

Disturbance at the Bee

Bees descended on the room where the geography bee was underway. Chaos broke out. All the answers were being shouted out but weren't matched to any questions.

- Is more or less than half of Africa in the southern hemisphere?

- The war in Vietnam spread to what two neighboring countries?

- Where did thousands of people move in 1848 in hopes of finding gold?

- What country controls the Panama Canal?

- What city is sacred to Jews, Christians, and Muslims?

- What are the two official languages of Canada?

- Where was a wall built to divide east from west?

- Shinto is a religion of what country?

The Mystery:

WHICH ANSWERS ARE *NOT* CORRECT FOR ANY OF THE QUESTIONS?

U.S.   Panama   Japan   China

BERLIN   CANADIAN   French

ENGLISH   MORE   LESS

Jerusalem   AFRICA   LONDON

CALIFORNIA   LAOS   INDIA   Cambodia

Name_____

Switched Suitcases

In a crowded airport, someone switches suitcases with Rosco. Is it an accident? Or is it the scent of Limburger cheese in Rosco's suitcase that lured someone (maybe another rat) to steal it? Whatever the reason, he is missing his prized possessions!

Though the suitcases are identical in kind, the stickers show that the two travelers have been to different places.

The Mystery:

WHAT COUNTRY OR COUNTRIES HAVE BOTH TRAVELERS VISITED?

THE OUTBACK

Mt. Ebert

Angor Wat

Brandenburg Gate

Transylvania

PILLARS OF HERCULES

Khyber Pass

MT. FUJI

Sydney Opera House

Holy See

Okefenokee Swamp

Land of Fire & Ice

Name_____

Geography Mysteries—Learning Adventures Series

The Hijacked Venom

It was probably foolish of Rosco to try to combine a Mediterranean cruise and an important delivery of frozen cobra venom to a lab in Istanbul. The temptation was just too great for a pair of international thieves on the same cruise.

And so, somewhere between the coast of Syria and the island of Cypress, it happened: the freezer of valuable cobra venom was hijacked.

A fast boat took off, heading for the coast of Turkey. Rosco watched in agony as the freezer sped away. Before long, however, he was in hot pursuit of the cold case.

Luckily, Rosco could intercept the thieves' communications and hear where they were going. He heard them describe their route by sea from

Turkey to Crete
to Montenegro
to Tunisia
to Mallorca
to Monaco
to Sardinia
to Morocco.

He followed, traveling these directions:

southwest, northwest, south and east, northwest, northeast, southwest, and southwest again.

The Mystery:

DID ROSCO TRAVEL IN THE RIGHT DIRECTIONS TO STAY ON THE TRAIL OF THE VENOM THIEVES?

Name_____

Lost in Lost Valley

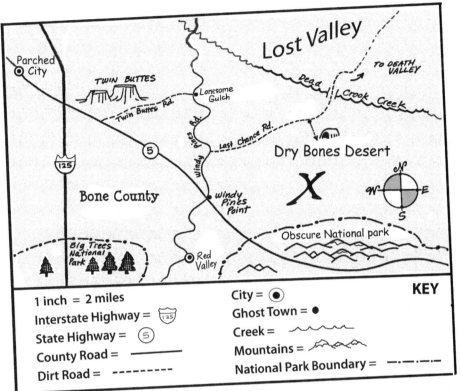

Rosco didn't think he needed to bother with a map when he went to visit some old ghost towns. That explains why he is now lost in Lost Valley. (See the **X** on the map for his location.)

He wanders north across Last Chance Road to Dead Crook Creek, northwest along the creek, and south on Windy Pines Road to Red Valley. From there he heads directly west through the national park until he hits Highway 125. Here he catches a ride to Parched City, where a worried Boomerang is waiting for him.

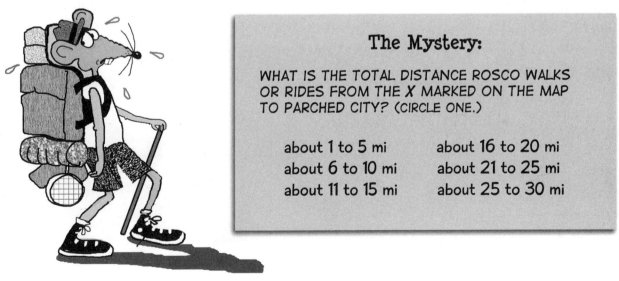

The Mystery:

WHAT IS THE TOTAL DISTANCE ROSCO WALKS OR RIDES FROM THE **X** MARKED ON THE MAP TO PARCHED CITY? (CIRCLE ONE.)

about 1 to 5 mi   about 16 to 20 mi

about 6 to 10 mi   about 21 to 25 mi

about 11 to 15 mi   about 25 to 30 mi

Name_____

The Hasty Leap

Rosco shows off his cannonball form at lakes all over the world. Today he is taking the leap into one of the world's great lakes, without stopping to check the water conditions. (This is a bad idea, Rosco!) Let's hope he is not jumping into Boiling Lake.

This particular lake is in a country that borders a sea, a large gulf, and an ocean. It is located south of the Tropic of Cancer. It is one of the lakes Rosco has on his list:

I LOVE TO MAKE A SPLASH!

Lake Superior
Lake Nios
Lake Maricaibo
Lake Baikal
Boiling Lake
Lake Chapala
Lake Tanaganyika
Lake Texococo
Lake Titicaca
Lake Victoria
Lake Tahoe

The Mysteries:

WHICH COULD BE THE LAKE (OR LAKES) FOR THIS JUMP?

WHICH OF THESE LAKES HAS ACTUALLY EXPLODED?

Name_____

80 ©Incentive Publications, Inc., Nashville, TN

Trouble on the Ice

As Rosco is enjoying a leisurely afternoon of skating on a frozen river, trouble erupts. Some prankster whizzes by and grabs his hat. Rosco races after the culprit. A crash ensues, and the trouble leads to a hospital emergency room in the nearest town.

Rosco's skating fiasco takes place at approximately this location:

41°38'N, 72°3'W

THIS IS ALL YOUR FAULT!

The Mysteries:

ON WHAT RIVER IS ROSCO SKATING?

IS THIS NORTH OF THE ARCTIC CIRCLE?

WHAT TOWN IS PROBABLY THE PLACE WHERE THE HOSPITAL IS LOCATED?

THAT'S RIGHT! BLAME ME FOR YOUR OWN CLUMSINESS!

Name_____

The Great Cheeseburger Search

Guess what happens after Rosco reads an article titled, **"15 Cheeseburgers You Must Eat Before You Die"**? Right! He decides he must try every one of them.

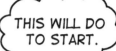

Here are the restaurants on the list. Rosco gets to every one of these cities, and tests all the burgers—some of them more than once.

- Le Tub, in Hollywood, FL

- Dick's Drive-In, in Seattle, WA

- Penguin Drive-In, in Charlotte, NC

- Billy Goat Tavern, in Chicago, IL

- Ted's Montana Grill, in Atlanta, GA

- Bobcat Bite, in Las Vegas, NV

- Louis' Lunch, in New Haven, CT

- Burger Joint, in San Francisco, CA

- Cherry Cricket, in Denver, CO

- Rouge, in Philadelphia, PA

- Peter Luger Steak House, in Brooklyn, NY

- Keller's Drive-In, in Dallas, TX

- Arctic Road Runner, in Anchorage, AK

- Murder Burger Drive Inn, in Davis, CA

- Port of Call, in New Orleans, LA

The Mystery: HOW MANY OF THESE BURGERS ARE FOUND IN CAPITAL CITIES?

Name_____

Time Trickery

When they stop to think about it, Rosco and Boomerang realize that time travel actually is possible. They can jump backward or forward a whole day, just by crossing the International Date Line. Rosco also realizes that they will be crossing the Date Line several times on this trip to various places in the Pacific.

- They leave Samoa at noon on Sunday, traveling one hour to Tonga.

- They leave Tonga at 5:00 PM on Tuesday and fly three hours to eastern Australia.

- They leave Australia at 11:00 AM on Thursday and fly three hours to Fiji.

- They leave Fiji at 9:00 AM on Saturday and fly four hours to Hawaii.

The Mysteries:

WHEN DO ROSCO AND BOOMERANG ARRIVE IN TONGA?

WHEN DO ROSCO AND BOOMERANG ARRIVE IN AUSTRALIA?

WHEN DO ROSCO AND BOOMERANG ARRIVE IN FIJI?

WHEN DO ROSCO AND BOOMERANG ARRIVE IN HAWAII?

(GIVE A TIME AND DAY AS THE SOLUTION TO EACH MYSTERY.)

Name_____

Shocking News

Rosco is often amazed by news from around the world. Today is no exception. As he reads his five daily newspapers, he thinks about which of these shocking stories he would most like to observe.

Daily Tidings————Friday, May 6
LLAMA TRAPPED IN ELEVATOR IN OSLO

Evening Gazette———Friday, May 6
Flying Sleigh Spotted at 0°N, 0°E

Sun City Times.........Fri., May 6th
Crocodile Swallows Volkswagen in Bissau

Friday, May 6————City Post
TALKING LIZARD PERFORMS IN RANGOON

Evening News.........Friday, May 6
Helicopters Steal All Auckland Parking Meters

Rat Quarterly

The Mystery:

WHERE DOES EACH OF THESE SHOCKING STORIES TAKE PLACE?

Name_____

84

History Mysteries

Geography plays a huge role in world history. Rosco can match up the countries with these history mysteries. Can you?

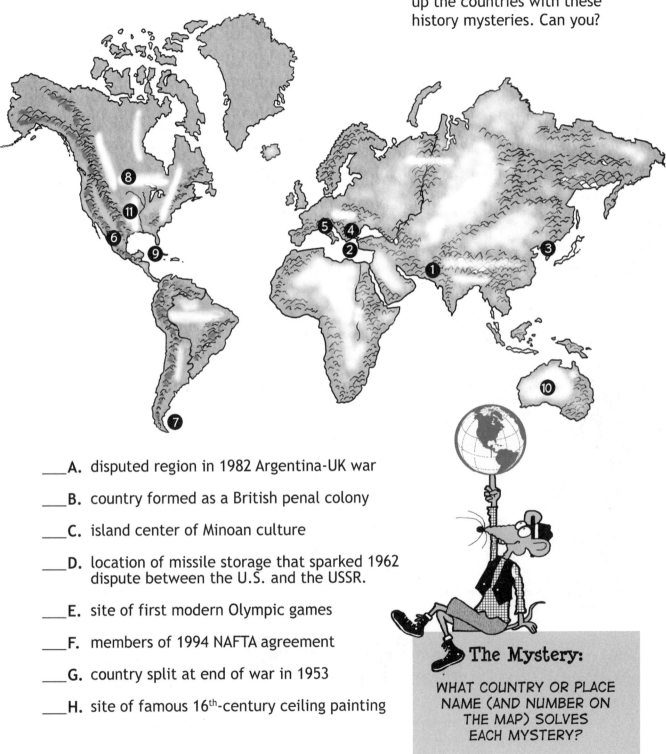

___A. disputed region in 1982 Argentina-UK war

___B. country formed as a British penal colony

___C. island center of Minoan culture

___D. location of missile storage that sparked 1962 dispute between the U.S. and the USSR.

___E. site of first modern Olympic games

___F. members of 1994 NAFTA agreement

___G. country split at end of war in 1953

___H. site of famous 16th-century ceiling painting

The Mystery:

WHAT COUNTRY OR PLACE NAME (AND NUMBER ON THE MAP) SOLVES EACH MYSTERY?

Name_____

Hooked on Travel

Fishing has immediate rewards—especially for a fishing expert like Boomerang. Because he always wants to hook more interesting and tasty rewards, he tries out some of the world's greatest rivers:

Amazon	MacKenzie
Yangtze	Indus
Danube	Nile
Euphrates	Ob
Ganges	Mississippi

The Mystery:

WHEN BOOMERANG VISITS THE MOUTH OF EACH OF THE RIVERS ON THE LIST, WHICH OF THESE BODIES OF WATER IS HE NOT LIKELY TO SEE?

Atlantic Ocean	East China Sea	Black Sea
Persian Gulf	Bay of Bengal	Arctic Sea
South China Sea	Arabian Sea	Mediterranean Sea
Gulf of Mexico	Hudson Bay	Sea of Japan

Name_____

Going to Extremes

The world is a grand collection of extremes. Rosco wants to see them all. This is because he has learned that the world's extremes become tourist attractions, and tourist attractions usually have refreshment stands.

JUST ENOUGH TIME FOR A LITTLE SIESTA BEFORE I SAIL INTO THE WORLD'S BUSIEST SEAPORT!

He takes a tour of these astonishing extremes:

the world's busiest seaport
the world's longest undersea tunnel
the world's longest fjord
the "Roof of the World"
the world's most densely populated country
the world's biggest glacier

The Mystery:

WHEN ROSCO TAKES THIS TOUR (ABOVE), WILL HE BE ON CONTINENTS WHERE HE CAN ALSO SEE ALL OF THESE EXTREMES?

- the world's largest island
- the world's longest suspension bridge
- the world's longest collection of coral reefs
- the world's largest mud building

Name_____

The Arachnid Capers

A particularly sinister group of characters carried off a series of robberies known as "The Arachnid Capers." They collect dangerous spiders and use them to frighten people. With a venomous spider held over their heads, victims are more than willing to give up treasured food, jewelry, secrets, codes, electronics, and money.

The collection of spiders includes:

- **Brazilian wandering spiders from: $9°N$, $79°W$**

- **redback spiders from: $25°S$, $125°E$**

- **tree-dwelling funnel-web spiders from: $30°S$, $132°E$**

- **brown recluse spiders from: $36°N$, $98°W$**

- **black widow spiders from: $46°N$, $121°W$**

(Fortunately, police caught up with the suspects before any real harm was done. Rosco was recruited to help return the spiders to their native habitats.)

I MUST BE CRAZY TO DO THIS JOB! I STILL GET NIGHTMARES FROM MY ENCOUNTER WITH THE GOLIATH BIRDEATER TARANTULA!

The Mystery:

FROM WHAT PLACES WERE THE SPIDERS COLLECTED?

Name_____

88

Crowded Conditions

When thousands of angry mice storm an area that Rosco is visiting, he's eager to discover the reason. The problem is—the territory that has been home to the mice is now so crowded with hordes of people that the mice have to move. It's no wonder things are crowded; this is one of the most densely-populated areas of the world.

The Mysteries:

WHICH OF THESE COULD BE THE AREA OF THE WORLD WHERE ROSCO ENCOUNTERED THE MICE: Nunavut, Canada; along the Nile River; central Australia; western Europe; northern Russia; or Hong Kong?

WHAT IS THE WORLD POPULATION AT THIS MOMENT? (Visit the world population clock on the Internet at *www.census.gov/main/www/popclock.html*.)

CHECK THE POP CLOCK IN HALF AN HOUR. WHAT IS THE WORLD POPULATION NOW?

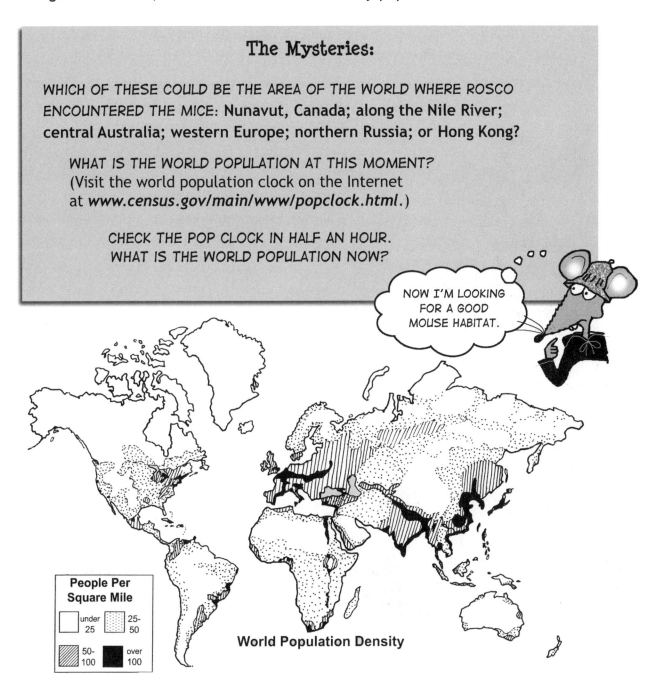

NOW I'M LOOKING FOR A GOOD MOUSE HABITAT.

People Per Square Mile

under 25 | 25-50 | 50-100 | over 100

World Population Density

Name_____

Captured in the Channel

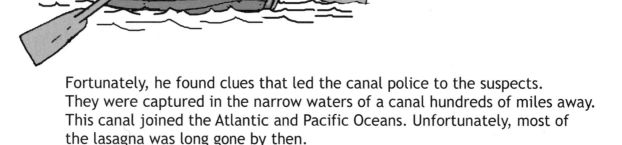

AH, THE LINGERING AROMAS OF RICOTTA, MOZZARELLA, AND PARMESAN CHEESE!

The narrow waters of a canal provide a convenient place to trap a ship. One group of crafty characters managed to trap three freighters in one week—all in different canals. Each time, they made off with hundreds of pounds of frozen lasagna.

Rosco, well-known cheese connoisseur, came along to check out the sites of the crimes. He snooped around in the three canals in this order: a canal joining Lake Superior with Lake Huron, a canal joining Lake Huron with Lake Erie, and a canal joining Lake Erie with the Hudson River.

Fortunately, he found clues that led the canal police to the suspects. They were captured in the narrow waters of a canal hundreds of miles away. This canal joined the Atlantic and Pacific Oceans. Unfortunately, most of the lasagna was long gone by then.

The Mysteries:

WHAT THREE CANALS DID ROSCO VISIT TO HUNT FOR CLUES (IN THE ORDER OF HIS VISITS)?

IN WHAT CANAL WERE THE LASAGNA THIEVES CAPTURED?

Name_____

90

The Disappearing Dogs

REWARD

for information leading to the recovery of stolen cheese dogs

Call Rosco - 555-Ratt

CHEESE-DOG LOVERS OF THE WORLD HAVE TO STICK TOGETHER!

Just as Rosco is making a list of things he plans to do on his trip around the U. S., he hears that a calamity has occurred in ten states. All the cheese dogs have disappeared—not just some cheese dogs, but ALL the dogs in the entire state in all ten states!

Rosco, the great fan of a good cheese dog, rushes to these states to see if he can help solve the mystery of the disappearing dogs. (He wants to be around when the dogs are located!) These are the states:

Wisconsin
Nevada
Florida
Pennsylvania
Kansas
Oklahoma
Maine
Idaho
California
North Carolina

Rosco's List
Things to Do in the U.S.

1. Eat freshly-caught Atlantic lobster.
2. Sail on two Great Lakes.
3. Visit Mt. Rushmore.
4. Hike through the Cumberland Gap.
5. Paddle on the Great Dismal Swamp.
6. Ride across the Dust Bowl.
7. Cross Tornado Alley.
8. See Death Valley.
9. Bike around the Great Basin.
10. Raft on the Snake River.
11. Explore Glacier National Park.

The Mystery:

WHICH THINGS ON HIS LIST WILL ROSCO BE ABLE TO DO IN THE STATES WITH THE MISSING HOT DOGS?

Name_____

Copycat Crimes

Rosco finds his curiosity piqued by the case of the copycat crimes. It seems that wherever a crime was committed, within a week some copycat repeated that same crime at the exact opposite location on the globe. (For instance, a crime at **14°N, 17°W** was repeated at **14°S, 17°E**.)

Here are the curious crimes:

Holes were drilled in a huge vat of enchilada sauce, emptying the vat in Encinitas, CA, U.S.A. at **33°N, 117°W**.

All the parrots were released from their cages in Sao Louis, Brazil at **25°S, 44°W**.

The garbage cans outside every building were suddenly filled with greasy chicken wings in the Maldives at **0°, 73°E**.

All the snowmobiles on the central east coast of Greenland disappeared at **74°N, 25°W**.

An upside-down screeching cat image appeared on all the computer screens in Punta Arenas, Chile at **53°S, 70°W**.

Dozens of boats in the area of Hawaii around **19°N, 155°W** were overturned.

THERE'S GOT TO BE A REASONABLE EXPLANATION FOR THIS!

The Mystery:

WHAT COPYCAT CRIME TOOK PLACE IN EACH OF THESE LOCATIONS?

   A. Coral Sea

   B. Southern Colombia

   C. Southwestern Australia

   D. Antarctica

   E. Southern Somalia

   F. Kazakhstan

Name_____

Confusion in the Mess Hall

Rosco was invited to greet the troops at seven overseas U.S. military bases. He arrived at each of these countries by boat: Crete, England, Ecuador, Japan, Spain, Guam, and Germany.

When he arrived at the first base, Rosco was told that a battalion of soldiers at each base was being deployed to Turkey. Rosco didn't hear the information quite right.

He thought he had been asked to "destroy the turkey." He assumed that the turkey must be hazardous to the health of the troops.

Rosco took his mission seriously and found all the turkey in the kitchen of every mess hall. He personally carried all turkey dinners, sandwiches, soup, and sausages to the garbage, causing much confusion in each mess hall.

The Mystery:

AT EACH STOP, ROSCO'S BOAT DOCKED ON THE EDGE OF A PARTICULAR BODY OF WATER. WHICH OF THESE WOULD *NOT* BE ON THE LIST OF PLACES WHERE HE DOCKED?

- Pacific Ocean
- Baltic Sea
- Black Sea
- Bay of Biscay
- Gulf of Aden
- Libyan Sea
- Caribbean Sea
- Irish Sea
- Sea of Japan
- North Sea

WHAT A FAUX PAS! I THINK THE ONLY TURKEY AROUND HERE IS ME!

Name_____

Pranks on the Premises

A rash of troublesome pranks is plaguing Lord Puddleton's Estate. (Purely by coincidence, this happens while Rosco is a guest there.) In a period of just three days, the host finds:

- whipped cream on windows of the room just north of the center stable.

- hundreds of spiders stuck in molasses on the structure farthest south of the vegetable garden.

- spaghetti hanging from chandeliers in the first room southwest of the kitchen.

- a greased floor in the second room east of the terrace.

- gallons of Jello in all the sinks in the first room directly east of the caretaker's apartment.

- the feature just east of the Japanese garden filled with a thousand ping pong balls.

The Mysteries:

Where . . .

1. IS THE JELLO?

2. ARE THE SPIDERS?

3. IS THE SPAGHETTI?

4. IS THE GREASED FLOOR?

5. ARE THE PING PONG BALLS?

6. IS THE WHIPPED CREAM?

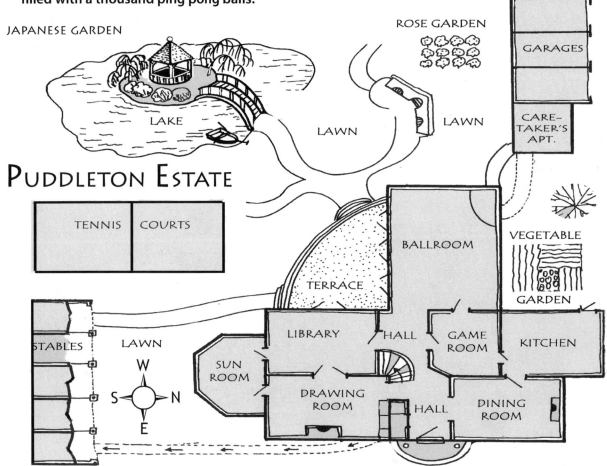

PUDDLETON ESTATE

Name_____

The Snatched Sandwich

Nothing is quite as important to Rosco as being prepared when he travels. He often brings his own food—just in case the food supply should be poor in the new location.

On his trip to the Canary Islands, he carries a special lunchbox of sandwiches that he hopes will last for a few days. Imagine his distress when, as soon as he steps off the plane, the lunchbox is snatched from his hands and disappears from his sight!

Slabs of cheddar, chunks of gouda, globs of pimento cheese, crumbs, and other clues are found in several locations. They are:

- **the Dardanelles**
  - **the Galapagos Islands**
    - **Malta**
      - **the Windward Islands**
        - **Sri Lanka**

As reports come in, Rosco consults his world map and ponders which clues to follow. He decides that he must track down all the leads. This means traveling to each of the five places where clues have been found.

The Mysteries:

1. IF ROSCO STARTS WITH THE LOCATION THAT IS CLOSEST TO THE CANARY ISLANDS, WHERE WILL HE GO FIRST?

2. IF ROSCO STARTS WITH THE LOCATION THAT IS FARTHEST FROM THE CANARY ISLANDS, WHERE WILL HE GO FIRST?

Name_____

A Spontaneous Trip

Rosco's pet goldfish has vanished! She always said she wanted to see the world. Rosco supposes she may have hitched a ride on the bottled water delivery truck that often comes down his alley.

Suppose that the goldfish did go on a trip. Assume that the goldfish left without warning because she got an opportunity to swim in one of the world's great bays.

Keep assuming that the goldfish gets her wish and right now is happily splashing and leaping around in waters that are north of the equator, are surrounded by one country, and are connected by a strait to the Atlantic Ocean.

I HOPE MY PAL, BOOMERANG THE CAT, DIDN'T HAVE ANYTHING TO DO WITH GOLDIE'S UNEXPECTED DEPARTURE.

The Mystery:

WHICH BAY COULD THIS BE?

- Bay of Bengal
- Shark Bay
- Hudson Bay
- Lamon Bay
- Maunalua Bay
- Bay of Biscay

Name_____

The Dreaded Triangle

Strange things happen in the Bermuda Triangle (also known as the Devil's Triangle)—an imaginary area of the Atlantic Ocean with endpoints at Bermuda; Miami, Florida; and San Juan, Puerto Rico. Supposedly, many sea vessels and aircraft have mysteriously disappeared in this area—never to be found.

Various theories attempt to explain the mysteries. Some even blame space aliens or sea monsters. Though scientists agree that the area has unusual characteristics, most believe that there are reasonable explanations for the incidents. Whatever the science says, Rosco wishes to stay away from this dreaded area.

The Mysteries:

RESEARCH THE STORY OF FLIGHT 19. DISCUSS IT WITH SOME FRIENDS AND COME UP WITH YOUR OWN THEORY.

IF HE DOES NOT WISH TO VISIT THE BERMUDA TRIANGLE, WHICH OF THESE LOCATIONS SHOULD ROSCO AVOID?

A. 25°N, 70°W   G. 23°N, 80°W

B. 18°N, 55°W   H. 26°N, 66°W

C. 20°S, 13°E   I. 18°N, 70°E

D. 28°N, 72°W   J. 19°N, 68°W

E. 25°N, 81°W   K. 15°N, 85°W

F. 38°N, 58°W   L. 15°S, 80°E

I SHOULD KNOW BETTER THAN TO WATERSKI IN THE BERMUDA TRIANGLE!

Name_____

The Last Question

It's down to the last question in the final round of the geography bee. Rosco is still in the competition! In fact, the other contestant has just missed a question. If Rosco gets this one right, it will be the last question—and he will win!

THIS "BEE" IS IN THE BAG!

The question:

Eight of these questions have a "no" answer. Which ones are they?

1. Is the Dead Sea really completely dead?
2. Is Easter Island a center for raising Easter bunnies?
3. Are there really devils in Tasmania?
4. Could you ride a train across Lake Pontchartrain?
5. Has Niagara Falls ever stopped flowing?
6. Are there tombstones in the "Graveyard of the Atlantic"?
7. Are you likely to find females in Male?
8. Is Cape Hatteras shaped like a hat?
9. Is it ever chilly in Chile?
10. Can you swim in El Mirage Dry Lake?
11. Is a wombat designed to use for hitting baseballs?
12. Does someone own the North Pole?

The Mystery:

HOW SHOULD ROSCO ANSWER THIS QUESTION IN ORDER TO WIN THE GEOGRAPHY BEE?

Name_____

The Last Mystery

Wherever Rosco travels, he is always delighted to return home to New York City. This city has endless miles of back alleys, streets, and trashcans to explore—305 square miles of land area in all. What's even better: his own home garbage can is a secret entrance to the thousands of miles of underground tunnels that hold sewers, cables, pipes, utility lines, and subway tracks. Rosco will take you to some of his above-ground favorite places—but you might have to take an underground route to get there!

IT'S A BEAUTIFUL DAY IN MY NEIGHBORHOOD.

#12 Rosco Rat

Rosco's New York City Favorites:

Metropolitan Museum of Art
Bronze Charging Bull statue
China Town
Billy's Bakery (Manhattan)
Brooklyn Bridge
Times Square

Coney Island
Grimaldi's Pizzaria (Brooklyn)
Grand Central Station
Ground Zero
La Cheesecake Bakery (Queens)
Statue of Liberty

The Mystery:

A MYSTERY DEVELOPS AS ROSCO SHOWS YOU AROUND NEW YORK. WHAT IS THAT MYSTERY? YOU MUST CREATE IT. GET A MAP OF THE CITY OR ANY OTHER TOOLS YOU NEED, AND WRITE THE LAST MYSTERY. USE GEOGRAPHY SKILLS AND SOME OF ROSCO'S FAVORITE PLACES IN YOUR MYSTERY.

YOU write it here:

Name_____

Geography Mysteries Checkup
Review and Assessment

Name _____ Date _____

You will need a copy of each of the four maps found on pages 106 to 109 in this book.

1. In their investigation of the theft of a valuable artifact, Rosco and his friend Boomerang are searching a coral island that completely encircles a lagoon. This shoreline feature is called

    a. a butte   d. a peninsula

    b. a spit   e. an atoll

    c. a sandbar   f. a glacier

2. Rosco's latest mystery takes him to a country bordered by France, Switzerland, and Austria. Most of the country is a long peninsula that extends into the Mediterranean Sea. What is the country?

3. Authorities have had trouble tracking a culprit in the wildernesses of the western United States. He is finally caught with his stash of stolen documents in the section of Mellowstone Park that has the greatest bear population. Where is the suspect found?

4. From this surveillance spot, Detective Rosco is watching a suspect who has holed up in a remote hut beside the Caribbean Sea. This particular tree could be located in any of the following countries except

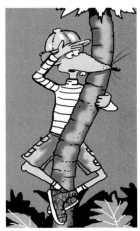

    a. Cuba   e. Costa Rica

    b. Guyana   f. Jamaica

    c. Ecuador   g. Panama

    d. Belize   h. Mexico

5. Rosco samples gourmet cheese delicacies at the sites of these cultural wonders:

    The Sphinx

    The Louvre

    Machu Picchu

    The Taj Mahal

    Stonehenge

    The Eiffel Tower

What continents will he visit?

6. A reliable sighting of a Yeti has been reported to local police. Rosco agrees to follow the lead into the mountains of Austria. What mountains will he be visiting?

    a. the Sierra Nevada Mountains

    b. the Alps

    c. the Andes Mountains

    d. the Carpathian Mountains

    e. the Himalayans

7. A shipwreck full of treasure has been found at this location:

26°N latitude, 62°W longitude

Could this be a ship that is in the Bermuda Triangle?

8. A search for a stolen prize cheese takes detectives to the Tropic of Cancer. Which country could they NOT be in?

a. Mexico   d. Algeria

b. Egypt   e. Saudi Arabia

c. Brazil   f. India

Morning Gazette - *May 12, 2011*

Stolen Gorillas Found in Somalia

City News - June 8, 2011

Scientist Disappears from Lab in Sierra Leone

The Mail Tribune July 5, 2011

Train Robbery Stuns Libyans

9. The mysteries in these news stories all take place on what continent?

10. The disappearance of a case of marshmallows should not be cause for international intrigue. But these marshmallows are a ruse to transport priceless jewels. A plane holding this treasure left Paris, France, at 8:15 PM on a Sunday. Police in Perth, Australia, got a tip that a mysterious plane would be landing there at 11:45 AM on the following day, Monday. How long (in time) was this flight?

11. A map has a scale of 2 centimeters = 1 kilometer. A bank robber with bags of money hijacked a helicopter in Sun City and flew it to a secret hideout in the tiny village of Hidden Cove. On the map, the two places are 19 centimeters apart. If the robber flew in a straight line between the city and the village, how far did she fly?

12. Someone has "borrowed" all the pastries from the kitchen of the Puddleton Estate. She and the pastries are hiding in a location that is just west of the library. Where are those pastries (if any are left uneaten)?

(Use the map of The Puddleton Estate.)

Shipwrecked in the Pailolo Channel. Don't want to go down with this gem. Use it well.

13. A bottle washed up on a shore in northern Oregon, U.S.A. It contained this message and a large diamond. Read the message and draw a conclusion about the location of the person who sent the message.

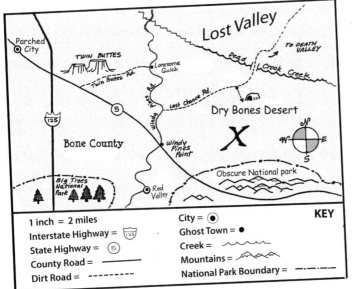

15. What major world river should Rosco travel to investigate a disaster at the Aswan Dam in Egypt?

16. Rosco chased a wanted spy across the Great Plains region of the United States. Which of these states would not be one he raced through on his motorcycle? *(Use the United States Physical Features Map.)*

    Iowa

    Kansas

    Idaho

    Nebraska

    Arizona

    Oklahoma

17. Rosco tracked down the world's best sour cream, triple-cheese cheesecake in the country on this list that does not border any of the other countries. Where did he find the luscious dish?

    a. Iraq   c. Turkey

    b. Iran   d. Bangladesh

14. Rosco is searching around Lost Valley for a stash of silver from an old train robbery. He's searched in Big Trees National Park. Now he will head for Dry Bones Desert. If he drives only on marked roads, which of these shows the direction sequence he must travel?

    a. NE, N, NE, S

    b. E, N, NE, SW, S

    c. N, SE, N, NW, SE

    d. N, SE, N, NE, S

    e. N, SE, N, NE, SE

18. A geography bee question almost stumps Rosco. But he thinks he's got the right answer. Does he?

Question: Which of these does not border Austria: Switzerland, Slovakia, Hungary, or Macedonia?

Rosco's answer: Macedonia

19. A tourist accidentally stumbles upon buried treasure near the base of a rock pillar which was isolated from a cliff due to wave erosion. This shoreline feature is called a

    a. stack   c. gulf

    b. plateau   d. dune

20. Lord Puddleton takes a stroll from the dining room, through the hall to the ballroom, and out the doors across the terrace to the path and over the bridge to the island. Is it correct to say that he walks in these directions (in this order)?

west, north, northwest

(Use the map of The Puddleton Estate.)

21. It's a bit risky to investigate a mystery from the sky. If Rosco's jump is successful, he'll land on the island of Vanuatu to pick up an important clue. If the jump goes well, in what world region will he land?

Oceania	Western Europe
Southeast Asia	Eastern Europe
Western Europe	Southwest Asia
South America	Africa
the Middle East	North or Central America

22. Crisscrossing the globe to solve a mystery, Rosco leaves Alaska at 1:00 AM on Wednesday and arrives in Japan five hours later. What day is it when he arrives in Japan?

23. The crime was a robbery of 12 dozen chocolate éclairs from a corner bakery. Where else would this happen but in a city that is the cultural center of France—a city full of tourists attracted to the great food, the art, the cathedrals, and the Eiffel Tower. What is this city?

24. A valuable emerald ring was hidden in a rocky cave on a mountainside. Before the thief could return to get it, the mountain erupted! This happened in the area of the world known as "the Ring of Fire." Could the location of this ring have been on Mt. Askja in Iceland? (Explain your answer.)

25. Which location can be found in Southeast Asia?

a. 40°S, 180°W   c. 38°N, 120°W
b. 16°N, 107°E   d. 30°S, 30°E

26. Rosco's not just surfing for fun. He's sneakily watching a suspect in an international surfboard theft ring. While riding waves off the east coast of Madagascar, Rosco is enjoying what body of water?

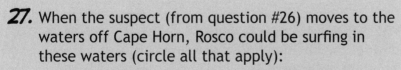

27. When the suspect (from question #26) moves to the waters off Cape Horn, Rosco could be surfing in these waters (circle all that apply):

a. Atlantic Ocean	e. Panama Canal
b. Caribbean Sea	f. Indian Ocean
c. Mediterranean Sea	g. Red Sea
d. Pacific Ocean	h. Black Sea

28. Once again, the suspect is elusive. Even Rosco is stymied this time. He's wandering around in the Ural Mountains. Which of these countries could be his current location? (Circle all that apply.)

a. Turkey   e. China

b. Italy   f. Kazakhstan

c. Russia   g. Iran

d. Finland   h. Spain

29. What rivers will a band of cattle thieves cross if they are escaping from the northwest corner of Washington on a straight-line route to the southwest corner of Louisiana? (Use the United States Physical Map.)

30. In his search for the world's best flatbread pizza, Rosco finds his taste satisfied in Yemen. Is he in the Middle East or Eastern Europe?

31. A volatile chemical has been recaptured from a band of international thieves. It is carefully transported by plane in a straight path from Sofia, Bulgaria, to Lisbon, Portugal. Will the plane pass over all three of these countries: Italy, Turkey, and Spain?

32. Rosco learns that a stash of missing gold coins is hidden in the famous stone circle, Stonehenge. To what country should he travel for the search?

33. Harbor police in a Sri Lankan port receive a tip that a missing freighter has turned up near the coast of Scotland. The location that came with the message is:

56°N latitude, 0° longitude

Should the police trust this tip?

34. The investigation of a missing diplomat takes Rosco to a narrow strip of land that connects two larger bodies of land. Where is he?

a. in a strait   c. in an oasis

b. on a cape   d. on an isthmus

35. Rosco spins the globe, closes his eyes, and touches a spot firmly to stop the spinning. So far, he has touched these spots:

| Peru | Borneo | Kenya | New Zealand |
| Cambodia | Namibia | Uruguay | New Guinea |

Which of these hemispheres has he not yet touched?

northern   eastern

southern   western

Mystery Record-Keeping Chart

Name_____

Directions: When you have completed the Mystery, write X over the number. When you are confident that you are comfortable with the concepts and processes used in the investigation, write X in the *Yes!* column.

#	Title	YES!	#	Title	YES!	#	Title	YES!
1	Long-Distance Pizza		31	Rat Overboard		61	Purloined Provolone	
2	Follow the Macaroni		32	Broken Promise		62	Intrigue in the Indies	
3	Fraudulent Paintings		33	Run Aground . . .		63	Geo-Clues	
4	Hidden Artifacts		34	Follow the Torch		64	Cover Up	
5	Vacation by the Sea		35	Au Gratin Sleuth		65	Distress in the . . .	
6	Race Against Time		36	Noodle in a . . .		66	Decoys	
7	Nacho Nabber		37	Frozen Message		67	Disturbance . . .	
8	Suspicious Cargo		38	Melted Clues		68	Switched Suitcases	
9	Abducted Scientist		39	Last Phone Call		69	Hijacked Venom	
10	Caught on Camera		40	Misplaced . . .		70	Lost in Lost Valley	
11	Jungle Secrets		41	Post-It Bandit		71	Hasty Leap	
12	Priceless Guitar		42	Furious Chase		72	Trouble on the . . .	
13	Curious Message		43	Phony Alibi		73	Great . . .	
14	Close to Home		44	Trouble at the . . .		74	Time Trickery	
15	Trekking to Treasure		45	Undelivered . . .		75	Shocking News	
16	Unasked Question		46	Itinerary Mix-Up		76	History Mysteries	
17	Stranded . . .		47	Pursuit of Pizza . . .		77	Hooked on Travel	
18	Emergency Delivery		48	Tough Question		78	Going to Extremes	
19	Missing Microchip		49	Extreme . . .		79	Arachnid Capers	
20	Elusive Recipe		50	Uninvited Guest		80	Crowded Conditions	
21	Space Stowaway		51	Backwards . . .		81	Captured in the . . .	
22	Vanished . . .		52	Lure of the . . .		82	Disappearing Dogs	
23	Coffee Caper		53	Fortune in a . . .		83	Copycat Crimes	
24	Suspects . . .		54	Fries . . .		84	Confusion in the . . .	
25	Cave Ciphers		55	Grass Skirt . . .		85	Pranks on the . . .	
26	Recovered . . .		56	Strange Stories		86	Snatched Sandwich	
27	Arachnid Encounter		57	Imposters on . . .		87	Spontaneous Trip	
28	Separated on the . .		58	Bumpy Flights		88	Dreaded Triangle	
29	Botched Train . . .		59	Million Dollar Fish		89	Last Question	
30	Imminent Eruptions		60	Undercover . . .		90	Last Mystery	

Geography Mysteries—Learning Adventures Series

World Time Zone Map

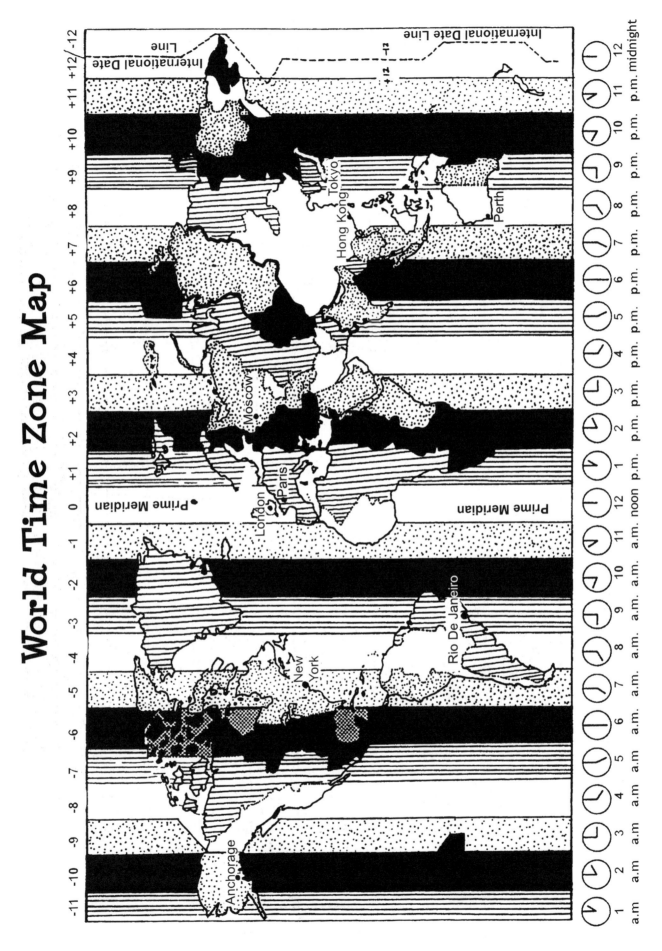

World Latitude and Longitude Map

United States Physical Map

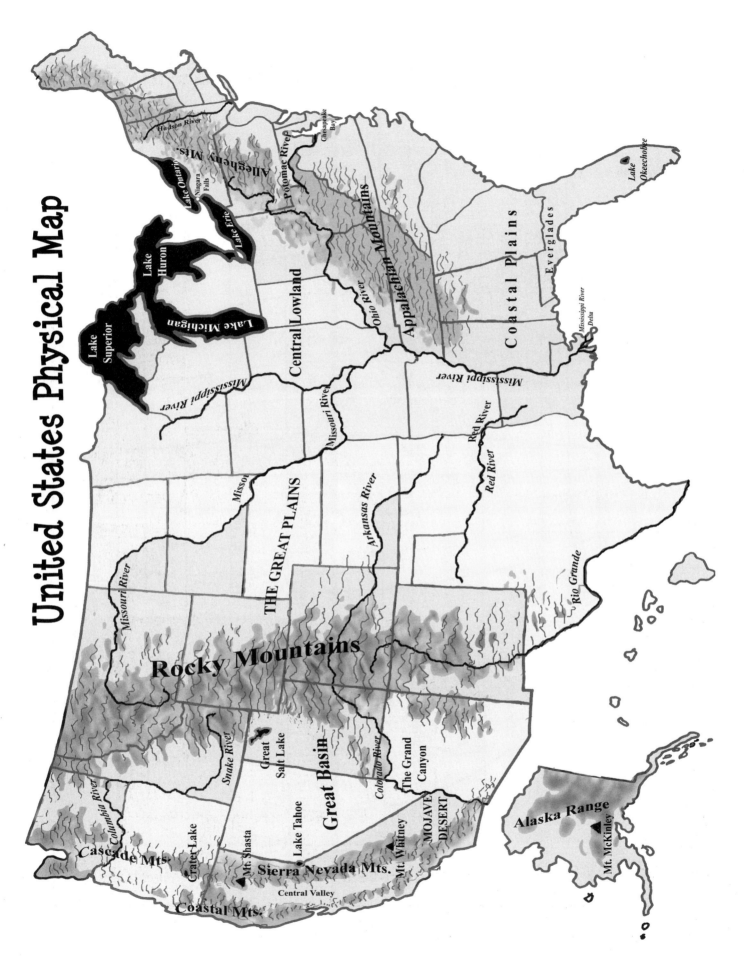

Hudson River

Allegheny Mts.

Lake Ontario
Niagara Falls
Lake Erie

Lake Huron

Lake Michigan

Lake Superior

Mississippi River

Chesapeake Bay

Potomac River

Ohio River

Appalachian Mountains

Central Lowland

Coastal Plains

Everglades

Lake Okeechobee

Mississippi River Delta

Mississippi River

Missouri River

Red River

Red River

THE GREAT PLAINS

Arkansas River

Rocky Mountains

Rio Grande

Missouri River

Columbia River

Snake River

Great Salt Lake

Great Basin

Lake Tahoe

Colorado River

The Grand Canyon

MOJAVE DESERT

Crater Lake

Mt. Shasta

Cascade Mts.

Sierra Nevada Mts.

Mt. Whitney

Central Valley

Coastal Mts.

Alaska Range

Mt. McKinley

The Puddleton Estate

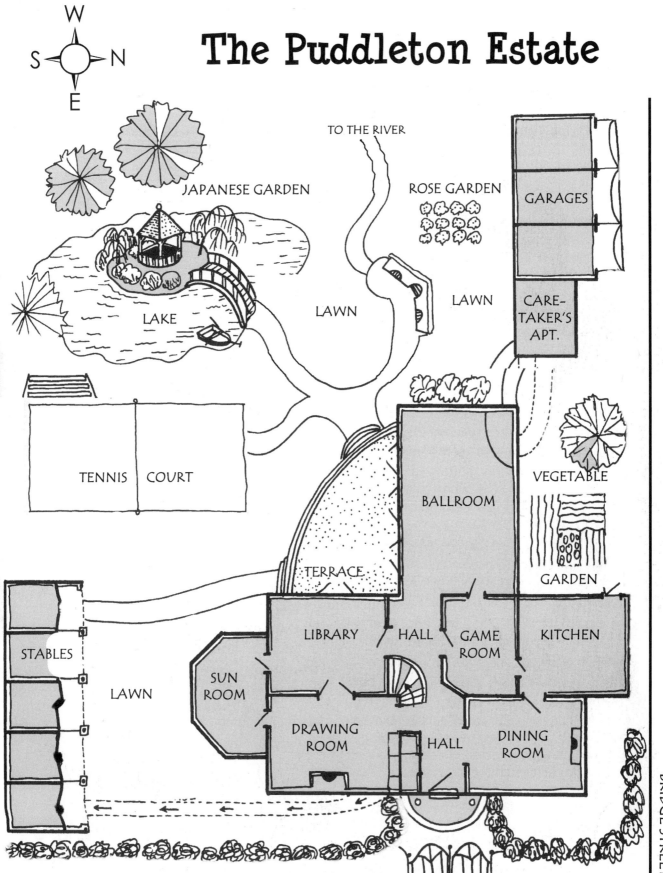

W N S E

TO THE RIVER

JAPANESE GARDEN

ROSE GARDEN

GARAGES

CARE-TAKER'S APT.

LAWN

LAWN

LAKE

VEGETABLE

TENNIS COURT

BALLROOM

GARDEN

TERRACE

STABLES

LIBRARY   HALL   GAME ROOM   KITCHEN

SUN ROOM

LAWN

DRAWING ROOM   HALL   DINING ROOM

BRIDGE STREET

PARK AVENUE

Answer Keys

The Geography Mysteries 1-90 (pages 10-99)

Mystery #1 (pg 10) Port Moresby (Papua New Guinea)

Mystery #2 (pg 11) May 1: Buenos Aires, Argentina; May 5: Sydney, Australia; May 8: Jakarta, Indonesia; May 14: Kingston, Jamaica; May 18: Kinshasa, Democratic Republic of Congo (or Brazzaville, capital of the Republic of Congo); May 22-Naples, Italy

Mystery #3 (pg 12) Paintings are picked up at: 5-Palais Royale; 1-Sacré-Coeur; 7-Notre Dame; 9-Pantheon; 2-L'Arc de Triomphe; and A-Parc Citroën. The original was found at Sacré-Coeur.

Mystery #4 (pg 13) either the scrap of a priceless Persian tapestry OR the bronze statue of a Mesopotamian goddess

Mystery #5 (pg 14) Adriatic Sea

Mystery #6 (pg 15) Rosco reached the victim at 8:00 AM on Thursday, with five hours to spare.

Mystery #7 (pg 16) 10 (in addition to Guatemala) Honduras, Saint Lucia, Mexico, Venezuela, Brazil, Nicaragua, El Salvador, Haiti, Chile, Jamaica

Mystery #8 (pg 17) yes (The Confederation Bridge links Prince Edward Island with New Brunswick.) Other mysteries: Answers will vary.

Mystery #9 (pg 18) The White Nile River

Mystery #10 (pg 19) 1, 2, 5, 7, 8, 10; Check to see that the drawing shows one of these.

Mystery #11 (pg 20) There are no jungles in 5, 6, 16, or 19.

Mystery #12 (pg 21) Buyers from Bulgaria, Sweden, Hungary, Lithuania, and the United Kingdom do not have euros as their home currency. Other mysteries: These answers depend on the currency exchange rate between the euro and dollar and the euro and pound on the given day that students solve the mystery.

Mystery #13 (pg 22) Marshall Islands

Mystery #14 (pg 23) Anasazi Cliff Dwellings, Death Valley, Everglades National Park, Carlsbad Caverns, Alamo, Old Faithful

Mystery #15 (pg 24) 16,000 ft

Mystery #16 (pg 25) What is the point in Earth's orbit where it is farthest from the sun?

Mystery #17 (pg 26) Strait of Malacca

Mystery #18 (pg 27) 5; yes

Mystery #19 (pg 28) Accademia Gallery in Florence, Italy, under the toe of sculpture called "The David"

Mystery #20 (pg 29) b, e, f, g, i, j, n

Mystery #21 (pg 30) circle 4; North America, Europe

Mystery #22 (pg 31) the food supply (Cotopaxi—Ecuador)

Mystery #23 (pg 32) Ukraine (city of Odessa)

Mystery #24 (pg 33) the skier on Loon Loop just above the intersection of Loon Loop and Treacherous Trail

Mystery #25 (pg 34) Blue Caves of Volimes (Greece)

Mystery #26 (pg 35) Province of Nunavut

Mystery #27 (pg 36) rainforest areas of northern South America

Mystery #28 (pg 37) roving grizzly bears; year-round rainfall

Mystery #29 (pg 38) Bezdany Raid

Mystery #30 (pg 39) Mt. Etna, Italy, and Mt. Askja, Iceland, are not in the Ring of Fire area

Mystery #31 (pg 40) Tasman Sea

Mystery #32 (pg 41) 1. circle C, Idaho; 2. circle E, Maryland; 3. circle A, Missouri; 4. circle B, Tennessee; 5. circle D, Kansas

Mystery #33 (pg 42) Tierra del Fuego—off the southern tip of South America; Bahamas—in the Atlantic Ocean southeast of Florida and north of Cuba; Aegean Island—in the Aegean Sea off the tip of Greece; Solomon Islands—in the south Pacific Ocean east of Papua New Guinea; Aleutians—west of Alaska stretching toward Russia in the north Pacific Ocean. There may be shallow waters or atolls that cause ships to run aground.

110

Mystery #34 (pg 43) 15 (all but Belgium, Croatia, Lithuania, Slovakia, and Turkmenistan) Poland

Mystery #35 (pg 44) Persepolis (in Iran)

Mystery #36 (pg 45) Latvia

Mystery #37 (pg 46) Antarctica

Mystery #38 (pg 47) Indonesia, Maldives, Gabon, Somalia, Kiribati, Kenya, Colombia, Ecuador, and Uganda

Mystery #39 (pg 48) The last call from Hawaii. Rosco receives it at 7:15 PM, Monday, Hawaii time (12:15 AM, Tuesday, Rosco's home in New York)

Mystery #40 (pg 49) Circle these: the elliptical barge at the lower right corner of Khufu's tomb near the tombs of the queens; the farthest left tomb near the label "tombs of the nobles" below and left of The Great Sphinx; the tomb of the queen near the bottom of the map farthest to the right; the farthest left tomb beneath the label "tombs of the royal children"; and the Valley Temple that is just below the Great Sphinx.

Mystery #41 (pg 50) Missing: ET (Eiffel Tower) and TM (Taj Mahal) notes. ET belongs where LT is now. TM belongs where P-S is now. Two are still correctly placed: P-Pantheon and S-Stonehenge.

Mystery #42 (pg 51) strait, fjord, oasis, gulf

Mystery #43 (pg 52) At the time of the robbery, it was the middle of the night in Australia, not morning (12:30 AM to 1:30 AM). Also, it is NOT summer in July in Australia. School would not be out and it is unlikely that the family would be going to the beach.

Mystery #44 (pg 53) Cambodia

Mystery #45 (pg 54) Three: None were delivered to Africa, Northern Asia, or Oceania.

Mystery #46 (pg 55) Items on the Ireland list that belong on the Scotland list: 4, 7, 8; Items on the Scotland list that belong on the Ireland list: 1, 5, 7

Mystery #47 (pg 56) Pakistan and Oman

Mystery #48 (pg 57) Yes, Rosco is correct.

Mystery #49 (pg 58) 1. and 8. Antarctica; 2. Libya; 3. Kentucky, USA; 4. Austria; 5. Hawaii, USA; 6. Chile; 7. Greenland

Mystery #50 (pg 59) the stack

Mystery #51 (pg 60) The theft was discovered at 9 AM on Wednesday. The thief arrived in Arizona at midnight on Wednesday.

Mystery #52 (pg 61) 3, 5, 8, 19

Mystery #53 (pg 62) Lagunita Country Club in Caracas, Venezuela

Mystery #54 (pg 63) 1. Kaliningrad, Russia; 2. Pula, Croatia; 3. Land's End, England; 4. Komárom, Hungary and Slovakia

Mystery #55 (pg 64) Vanuatu, Barbados, Elba, Channel Islands

Mystery #56 (pg 65) Arctic Circle-2; Antarctic Circle-0; Tropic of Cancer-3; Tropic of Capricorn-2; Equator-4; Prime Meridian-3; International Date Line-2. *NOTE: Pay attention to the directions at the end of each story. In some cases, it is NOT the logical direction to follow.*

Mystery #57 (pg 66) Buenos Aires, Argentina (33°S latitude). Wellington, New Zealand is the capital farthest south at 41°S latitude.

Mystery #58 (pg 67) Sierra Madre Orientals, Atlas Mountains, and the Ural Mountains

Mystery #59 (pg 68) Check grids to see that correct fish are colored: the small fish with a black face that is in the horizontal 3 row; the eel that stretches across a part of row 5; and the lowest fish in the right-hand corner.

Mystery #60 (pg 69) Aruba; New Zealand; Murmansk, Russia; Egypt; Ho Chi Minh City, Vietnam; Vatican City; Bratislava, Slovakia; Belgrade, Serbia; and Vienna, Austria Budapest, Romani

Mystery #61 (pg 70) Chile, Nicaragua, Palau, Angola, Canada, Turkmenistan, Malaysia

Mystery #62 (pg 71) St. Lucia

Mystery #63 (pg 72) Rosco knows: 1. There are no typhoons in the Caribbean. Typhoons are only in the northwest Pacific Ocean. 2. There are no penguins in the Arctic. They are found only in Antarctica. 3. The aurora borealis cannot be seen from Costa Rica. 4. Maquiladoras factories are found only in Mexico.

Mystery #64 (pg 73) Iberian, Musandam, Yucatan, Balkan, Malay, Jutland, Scandinavian, Sinai

Mystery #65 (pg 74) Kalahari, Sahara, Arabian, Chihuahuan, Great Sandy (Mojave is out of the latitude range; Atacama and Namib are cool coastal deserts; Gobi, Patagonia, and Iranian are cold winter deserts.)

Mystery #66 (pg 75) Lake Okeechobee (Florida)

Mystery #67 (pg 76) Incorrect answers: U.S., China, Canadian, more, Africa, London, India

Mystery #68 (pg 77) Australia and United States

Mystery #69 (pg 78) yes

Mystery #70 (pg 79) about 15 to 20 mi

Mystery #71 (pg 80) Lake Chapala or Lake Texococo; Lake Nios has exploded.

Mystery #72 (pg 81) Connecticut River; no; Hanover, CT

Mystery #73 (pg 82) two (Atlanta and Denver)

Mystery #74 (pg 83)
arrives in Tonga at 1:00 PM on Monday;
arrives in Australia at 6:00 PM on Wednesday;
arrives in Fiji at 3:00 PM on Thursday;
arrives in Hawaii at 1:00 PM on Friday

Mystery #75 (pg 84) A. Norway; B. North Pole; C. Guinea-Bissau; D. Myanmar; E. New Zealand

Mystery #76 (pg 85) A. Falkland Islands (7); B. Australia (10); C. Crete (2); D. Cuba (9); E. Greece (4); F. Mexico (6), Canada (8), and USA (11); G. Korea (3); H. Italy (5)

Mystery #77 (pg 86) South China Sea, Hudson Bay, Sea of Japan

Mystery #78 (pg 87) No, the list includes sites in Europe, Asia, and Antarctica. The largest island is near North America, the longest coral reef is near Australia, and the largest mud buildings are in Africa.

Mystery #79 (pg 88) Brazilian: from Panama; redback from Australia; tree-dwelling funnel-web from Australia; brown recluse from Arkansas; black widow from Washington

Mystery #80 (pg 89) along the Nile River, Western Europe, Hong Kong; answers will vary for other mysteries

Mystery #81 (pg 90) Sault Ste. Marie Canal, Welland Canal, Erie Canal; the thieves were captured in Panama Canal.

Mystery #82 (pg 91) 1, 2, 4, 5, 6, 7, 8, 10 (9 is also allowed, as the Great Basin is sometimes defined as extending into Idaho.)

Mystery #83 (pg 92) A. overturned boats; B. garbage cans filled with chicken wings; C. flowing enchilada sauce; D. snowmobiles disappeared; E. parrots released; F. cat image on computer

Mystery #84 (pg 93) Black Sea, Gulf of Aden, Caribbean Sea

Mystery #85 (pg 94) 1. Jello—kitchen; 2. spiders—tennis court; 3. spaghetti—ballroom; 4. greased floor—drawing room; 5. ping pong balls—lake; 6. whipped cream—sun room

Mystery #86 (pg 95) 1. Malta; 2. Sri Lanka

Mystery #87 (pg 96) Hudson Bay

Mystery #88 (pg 97) A, D, E, H, J

Mystery #89 (pg 98) 1, 2, 4, 6, 8, 10, 11, 12

Mystery # 90 (pg 99) Mysteries will differ.

Answer Key

Geography Checkup (Assessment), pages 100-104

1. e
2. Italy
3. Green Lakes District
4. c
5. Africa, Asia, Europe, South America
6. b
7. no
8. c
9. Africa
10. 8½ hours
11. 9.5 km
12. on the Terrace
13. Hawaiian Islands
14. e
15. the Nile
16. Idaho, Arizona
17. d
18. yes
19. a
20. no; he would walk south, west, and southwest. (Note the compass rose.)
21. Oceania
22. Tuesday
23. Paris, France
24. no (the Ring of Fire surrounds the Pacific Ocean. Iceland is not in this area.)
25. b
26. the Indian Ocean
27. a, d
28. c, f
29. Columbia River, Snake River, Colorado River, Red River
30. Middle East
31. no (It will not pass over Turkey.)
32. England (or the United Kingdom)
33. yes (The latitude, longitude location is in the vicinity of Scotland.)
34. d
35. northern